Free Church Pastors in Germany – Perceptions of Spirit Possession and Mental Illness

Vouillot, L., Thelie, A. and Pollet, N. 2015. Comparison of T7E1 and surveyor mismatch cleavage assays to detect mutations triggered by engineered nucleases. *G3* 5(3), 407–15. doi:10.1534/g3.114.015834.

Wang, Z. P., Xing, H. L., Dong, L., Zhang, H. Y., Han, C. Y., Wang, X. C. and Chen, Q. J. 2015. Egg cell-specific promoter-controlled CRISPR/Cas9 efficiently generates homozygous mutants for multiple target genes in *Arabidopsis* in a single generation. *Genome Biology* 16(1), 144. doi:10.1186/s13059-015-0715-0.

Watanabe, K., Kobayashi, A., Endo, M., Sage-Ono, K., Toki, S. and Ono, M. 2017. CRISPR/Cas9-mediated mutagenesis of the *dihydroflavonol-4-reductase-B* (DFR-B) locus in the Japanese morning glory *Ipomoea (Pharbitis) nil*. *Scientific Reports* 7(1), 10028. doi:10.1038/s41598-017-10715-1.

Watanabe, K., Oda-Yamamizo, C., Sage-Ono, K., Ohmiya, A. and Ono, M. 2018. Alteration of flower colour in *Ipomoea nil* through CRISPR/Cas9-mediated mutagenesis of *carotenoid cleavage dioxygenase 4*. *Transgenic Research* 27(1), 25–38. doi:10.1007/s11248-017-0051-0.

Whinn, K. S., Kaur, G., Lewis, J. S., Schauer, G. D., Mueller, S. H., Jergic, S., Maynard, H., Gan, Z. Y., Naganbabu, M., Bruchez, M. P., O'Donnell, M. E., Dixon, N. E., van Oijen, A. M. and Ghodke, H. 2019. Nuclease dead Cas9 is a programmable roadblock for DNA replication. *Scientific Reports* 9(1), 13292. doi:10.1038/s41598-019-49837-z.

Winkelmann, T., Warwas, M., Raffeiner, B., Serek, M. and Mibus, H. 2016. Improved postharvest quality of inflorescences of *fbp1::etr1-1* transgenic *Burrageara* 'Stefan Isler lava flow'. *Journal of Plant Growth Regulation* 35(2), 390–400. doi:10.1007/s00344-015-9545-2.

Wolt, J. D., Wang, K. and Yang, B. 2016. The regulatory status of genome-edited crops. *Plant Biotechnology Journal* 14(2), 510–8. doi:10.1111/pbi.12444.

Wyman, C. and Kanaar, R. 2006. DNA double-strand break repair: All's Well That Ends Well. *Annual Review of Genetics* 40(1), 363–83. doi:10.1146/annurev.genet.40.110405.090451.

Xiong, J. S., Ding, J. and Li, Y. 2015. Genome-editing technologies and their potential application in horticultural crop breeding. *Horticulture Research* 2(February), 15019. doi:10.1038/hortres.2015.19.

Yamasaki, K., Kigawa, T., Inoue, M., Yamasaki, T., Yabuki, T., Aoki, M., Seki, E., Matsuda, T., Tomo, Y., Terada, T., Shirouzu, M., Tanaka, A., Seki, M., Shinozaki, K. and Yokoyama, S. 2005. Solution structure of the major DNA-binding domain of *Arabidopsis thaliana* ethylene-insensitive3-like3. *Journal of Molecular Biology* 348(2), 253–64. doi:10.1016/j.jmb.2005.02.065.

Zhang, B., Yang, X., Yang, C., Li, M. and Guo, Y. 2016. Exploiting the CRISPR/Cas9 system for targeted genome mutagenesis in petunia. *Scientific Reports* 6(1), 20315. doi:10.1038/srep20315.

Zhao, C., Shu, X. and Sun, B. 2017. Construction of a gene knockdown system based on catalytically inactive ("dead") Cas9 (dCas9) in *Staphylococcus aureus*. *Applied and Environmental Microbiology* 83(12). doi:10.1128/AEM.00291-17.

Zhou, H., Liu, B., Weeks, D. P., Spalding, M. H. and Yang, B. 2014. Large chromosomal deletions and heritable small genetic changes induced by CRISPR/Cas9 in rice. *Nucleic Acids Research* 42(17), 10903–14. doi:10.1093/nar/gku806.

Zhou, X., Jacobs, T. B., Xue, L. J., Harding, S. A. and Tsai, C. J. 2015. Exploiting SNPs for biallelic CRISPR mutations in the outcrossing woody perennial Populus reveals 4-coumarate:CoA ligase specificity and redundancy. *The New Phytologist* 208(2), 298–301. doi:10.1111/nph.13470.

Michael Grossklaus

Free Church Pastors in Germany – Perceptions of Spirit Possession and Mental Illness

PETER LANG
EDITION

Bibliographic Information published by the Deutsche Nationalbibliothek
The Deutsche Nationalbibliothek lists this publication in the Deutsche Nationalbibliografie; detailed bibliographic data is available in the internet at http://dnb.d-nb.de.

Library of Congress Cataloging-in-Publication Data
Names: Grossklaus, Michael, author.
Title: Free church pastors in Germany - perceptions of spirit possession and mental illness / Michael Grossklaus.
Description: New York : Peter Lang, 2016.
Identifiers: LCCN 2016045739 | ISBN 9783631698518
Subjects: LCSH: Pastoral psychology—Germany. | Spirit possession. | Mental illness—Religious aspects—Christianity. | Pastoral theology—Free churches. | Free churches—Germany.
Classification: LCC BV4012 .G76 2016 | DDC 253.5/20943—dc23 LC record available at https://lccn.loc.gov/2016045739

ISBN 978-3-631-69851-8 (Print)
E-ISBN 978-3-631-69852-5 (E-PDF)
E-ISBN 978-3-631-69853-2 (EPUB)
E-ISBN 978-3-631-69854-9 (MOBI)
DOI 10.3726/978-3-631-69852-5

Peter Lang Edition is an Imprint of Peter Lang GmbH.

Peter Lang - Frankfurt am Main · Bern · Bruxelles · New York · Oxford · Warszawa · Wien

This publication has been peer reviewed.

www.peterlang.com

Acknowledgements

Firstly I would like to thank the one without whom I would neither exist nor would have been able to write this thesis: Jesus Christ. Thank you for everything you have done for me and may this work and the associated results serve to appropriately help people who are in spiritual and mental need.

Thank you to everyone who has accompanied me along the way, to those who have lent me their support emotionally, professionally and financially. To those who encouraged me to keep going and to those who had to do without me because this work was on my heart. My wife Kerstin and my children Lea (14), Laura (11) and David (9) were especially affected. Even though it was not always easy for you – many thanks!

Thank you as well to my church who made it possible for me to write this research paper while still carrying out my diverse ministries. May God continue to richly bless the "Gnadenkirche" in Villingen, you are wonderful brothers and sisters.

I would also like to sincerely thank Dr. Yaseen Ally, my supervisor. His optimism encouraged me time and again to keep going and even though we could never personally shake hands, I would never have accomplished this without your help Yaseen. My wish for you is that you can guide many more students to a successful graduation – thank you!

My thanks also go to Hilary Griesshaber for supporting me with the translation; she devoted many hours to this and without her this thesis would not have been possible. God bless you richly for this!

Thanks are also due to my parents and my sister who always believed in me and provided me with as much support as possible.

Thanks also go to my Godmother Elfriede who died a few weeks ago at the age of 86 and who prayed much for me.

To my wonderful colleague and friend Isabel who knew I would reach my goal and who often encouraged me, thank you!

Thank you to all the pastors who allowed me to interview them, without your willingness to give information this thesis would not have come to be.

Thank you to the University of South Africa who made it possible for me to complete the studies over such a great distance.

SDG

Table of Contents

Foreword 11

Abstract 15

1 Psychology and Spirit Possession 17

1.1 What is Psychology? 17

1.1.1 What is the history of psychology? 20

1.2 What is mental illness? 24

1.3 How do psychologists diagnose mental illness? 27

1.3.1 General possibilities for diagnosis 27

1.3.2 DSM-5 and ICD-10 28

1.3.3 Further indications for the diagnosis of mental illness 28

1.3.3.1 The conviction of the psychologist towards the applied method 30

1.3.3.2 The therapist effect 30

1.3.3.3 Expectations of the client 30

1.3.3.4 Feedback 30

1.3.3.5 Medication 31

1.4 Cultural expressions of mental illness 31

1.5 Spirit possession from a psychological perspective 33

1.5.1 Culture-bound phenomenon 34

1.5.2 Witchcraft explanations 34

1.5.3 Hysteria and dissociation 34

1.5.4 Delusions 34

1.6 Interdisciplinary approach to spirit possession 38

1.6.1 The Anthropological Perspective 38

1.6.1.1 Natural explanations 38

1.6.1.2 Trance possession 39

1.6.1.3 Spirit possession without trance 39
1.6.2 The theological/historical perspective 39
1.6.3 The social-psychological perspective of Protestant and Catholic theologians 39
1.6.4 The medical-psychological perspective 39

2 Theology and Spirit Possession 41
2.1 What is Theology? 41
2.2 What is spirit possession? 43
2.3 Theological history of spirit possession 45
2.3.1 Antiquity, the Bible and early Christianity 45
2.3.2 The Middle Ages and Exorcism in the Catholic Church 47
2.3.3 The Time of Enlightenment 50
2.3.4 From the 19th Century Up to the 20th Century 51
2.3.5 Deliverance Ministry in the 21st Century 51
2.4 How do pastors diagnose spirit possession? 52
2.4.1 The Dilemma of free church pastors 53
2.5 Religious and cultural expression of spirit possession 54
2.6 Spirit possession in a theological-biblical perspective 55
2.6.1 Exorcism in the Old Testament 55
2.6.2 Exorcism in the New Testament 56

3 Psychological Theories of Spirit Possession 61
3.1 Hypnotism, hysteria and subconscious ideas 63
3.2 The psychodynamic theories of Sigmund Freud and Carl Gustav Jung 65
3.2.1 Sigmund Freud 65
3.2.2 Carl Gustav Jung 67
3.2.2.1 Spirit Possession 68
3.2.2.2 The Shadow 68
3.2.2.3 The Evil 69

3.2.3 Transpersonal Psychology ... 69
3.3 Organic psychiatric interpretations ... 70
3.3.1 Dissociative Disorders ... 70
3.4 Weak Quantum Theory ... 71
3.5 Model of Pragmatic Information ... 72
3.6 Parapsychological theory ... 74
3.6.1 History of Parapsychology ... 75
3.6.2 Current Status of Research ... 76
3.6.3 Criticism of parapsychological theory ... 77

4 Theological Theories of Spirit Possession ... 81
4.1 Theological Theories of Spirit Possession in the Protestant Churches in Germany ... 81
4.2.1 Dr. Kurt Koch ... 85
4.2.2 The Charismatic Movement within the Protestant Church ... 88
4.3 Theological Theories of Spirit Possession in the Catholic Churches in Germany ... 91
4.3.1 "Rituale Romanum" ... 92
4.3.2 Charismatic Movement within the Roman Catholic Church ... 95
4.4 Theological Theories of Spirit Possession in Free Churches in Germany ... 95
4.4.1 Bund evangelisch-freikirchlicher Gemeinden (BEFG) – Baptist Churches ... 97
4.4.2 Bund freier-evangelischer Gemeinden (BFEG) – Alliance of Free Protestant Churches ... 98
4.4.3 Bund freikirchlicher Pfingstgemeinden (BFP) – Alliance of Pentecostal Churches ... 98

5 Methodology ... 103
5.1 Research objective ... 103

5.2 Rationale 104
5.3 Design/Approach 105
5.3.1 Main characteristics on qualitative research 106
5.3.2 Interviews 107
5.3.3 Research Questions 108
5.3.4 Interview guide 109
5.4 Sampling 109
5.5 Participant demographics 110
5.6 Data collection using the semi-structured interviews 111
5.7 Thematic content analysis 112

6 Results and Discussion 115
6.1 Theme 1: Distinction between mental illness and spirit possession 115
6.1.1 Pastors who had treated and diagnosed spirit possession 119
6.1.2 Pastors who diagnosed mental illness 122
6.1.3 Pastors who are unsure 123
6.2 Theme 2: If it is a mental illness, how do they proceed? 123
6.3 Theme 3: If it is demon possession, how do they proceed? 124
6.4 Theme 4: Lack of integrated knowledge regarding mental illness and spirit possession 125

7 Conclusion 131

Reference List 135

Appendix 147
Appendix I 147
Appendix II 148

Foreword

This research work with the PhD as a goal had a beginning. This beginning lies several years back in the past. In order to understand the motivation and appreciate the intention of this thesis, some history will be briefly referred to. How did everything begin that was to end with the PhD?

One Saturday evening in 2004 I received a telephone call. A helper from a free church youth group called me to say I should come as soon as possible as there was a lady whose behaviour was very strange. He didn't want to go into any more detail on the phone, but I should immediately go to the church where she was.

At that point in time I was pastor of this free church and since I knew the caller I drove to our church immediately after the call. There I saw the woman cowering in a corner on the floor and when I spoke to her she turned her head to me. Her look was totally misplaced and I was more than shocked when she spoke to me with the voice of a young boy. I looked at the youth worker and he just said: *That is what I couldn't tell you on the phone.*

As of this day a counselling case began which changed my pastoral ministry as well as my world view because I was confronted with phenomena that I had never believed possible.

There are not enough pages here to describe everything that I experienced in the time that followed. I contacted many free church pastors, but none of them were familiar with what I had to report. Psychiatric institutions were also completely overwhelmed with this case. Was the woman possessed? Was she mentally ill? These questions came time and again and the answer was so hard to find.

Why could she speak in such different languages, why could she write with both her left hand and right hand, how could she play piano nearly perfectly when she had never learnt this? How could she know things that were impossible for her to know, that she could leave her body (demonstrably) and be insensitive to physical pain etc. Suddenly I was confronted with Satanism, ritual abuse and unbelievable experiences and the question became ever clearer: is this an expression of mental illness or spirit possession?

Against this background and some similar experiences with others who were seeking advice, I began, as a Free Church pastor, to search in the Bible and to deal intensively with the topic of Satan, demons, spirit possession, exorcism and deliverance ministry against a theological background. As well as reading the Bible, I read much literature on the topic. Some answers helped a little, others confused me.

Little by little I ventured into psychological literature and read about personality disorders, dissociative identity disorders, schizophrenia, demonological neuroses...

It became clear to me that my Christian faith and my theological knowledge seemed to be insufficient in cases such as these. It seemed to be not possible to 'pray away' everything, but first I had to acquire the psychological knowledge. Thus I became ever more aware of the specialist literature that was concerned with the experience and behaviour of people and I decided to begin to study psychology. At the end of the course for my master's degree at Lee University I wrote a thesis on the topic: *Holistic counselling in cases of paranormal phenomena*. I wanted to retrospectively research into what had happened, against a specialised background and using psychological knowledge. The course and the associated thesis broadened my theological horizon with psychological knowledge and this helped me immensely, and aided me to advance personally and in my vocation. I was involved with scientists at the IGPP in Freiburg, the leading European institution that has dealt with border areas of psychology for decades. Since this time the connection between theology and psychology has grown dear to me.

When it became possible for me to take a PhD course in psychology at UNISA, it was clear to me that the research project should also be dedicated to this particular group of themes. I wanted to investigate further into what possession phenomena were all about, that is how they can be demarcated from mental illnesses: *Free Church Pastors – Perceptions of Spirit Possession and Mental Illness* – this is the title of my PhD thesis. I was able to write the necessary research proposal for it in October 2013 and was then registered on the PhD programme.

Month by month I became more aware of the enormous challenge that this presented, but the goal was clearly defined and had three letters: P h D.

It was a great help for me that a supervisor was found from the University of South Africa (UNISA), Dr. Yaseen Ally, who himself had researched into witchcraft and was interested and motivated to accompany me over all the years up to the finished PhD thesis. I was his first PhD student and I found him to be very encouraging and competent as a supervisor. If it had been otherwise, an effective collaboration, without having even stood opposite each other, would not have been possible.

In the German psychology scene terms such as demons and spirit possession were and are not taken seriously by the majority – unfortunately. International professional circles see it differently, in a more differentiated way.

The question *mental illness or spirit possession?* continues to fascinate and the connection between theology and psychology is more than worthwhile; this I noticed not only in my pastoral ministry but also when giving counselling and therapy to people in a poor mental state.

Since I had hardly any help in 2004, I wanted to find out whether this was an isolated case or whether other Free Church pastors in Germany would fare similarly in this specific topic.

What was important to me, as well as the relevant specialised literature and my own previous research results, were the qualitative interviews with free church pastors. Their statements were to reveal to what extent they had concepts and were educated in order to effectively help people or not. It was clear to me that I would have to specifically choose free church pastors so as to be in accordance with the research topic.

While travelling to Africa on a two week trip in June 2015 I had the chance meet pastors in Uganda and Tanzania and to talk with them about this topic. It was also interesting to see how they specifically deal with this phenomenon.

All in all, the years of reading, contemplating and writing have made me personally more mature and I believe that the innumerable days and nights spent completing the doctoral thesis were worth it. An additional challenge was the fact that my mother tongue is German and not English, but this challenge was also not for nothing. Now the PhD thesis is completed and I wish and hope and believe that it is as it should be.

Abstract

In many cultures and religions of the world the belief in transcendental realities, like God, the Devil and other benevolent and malevolent spirits are widespread. These realities are constructed in different ways, depending upon context. In light of the development Western industrial societies have undergone, it follows that the belief in transcendental realities may have given way to beliefs that are steeped more, in empiricism. However, understanding the belief in transcendental realities seems to be gaining renewed interest in various social science disciplines in light of the fact that claims of experiences of spirit possession are escalating. The implication this understanding has on the treatment a patient receives is likely to depend upon the training of the practitioner consulted. It follows that the experiences of patients who believe they are possessed by a spirit is as equally important to practitioners of psychology as it is to theologians. Psychologists would likely ascribe a spirit possession to a psychological experience; while theologians will attest to the presence of a spiritual illness. This project focused on Free Church pastors in Germany and their perceptions of spirit possession and mental illness. To explore Free Church pastors' understanding of spirit possession and mental illness is critical in light of the overlap of symptoms. Misdiagnosis may result in a client receiving treatment which may not be appropriate. Interviews with Free Church pastors were conducted. The results were analysed and four themes were identified.

Based on these interviews conclusions could be drawn which ultimately made it clear that the German free church pastors' theological training needs to be supplemented in the area of psychology and that the pastors are unable to cope in the area of 'spirit possession or mental illness'.

Key words: mental illness; spirit possession; psychology; theology; Free Church pastors; exorcism

1 Psychology and Spirit Possession

This chapter focuses on the psychological interpretation and understanding of spirit possession. Specifically, the aim is to elucidate the dominant approaches to the diagnosis of mental illness as well as the ways in which a spirit possession is understood.

1.1 What is Psychology?

William James, one of the pioneers of psychology as a scientific discipline, once stated "nasty little subject – all one cares to know lies outside" (Simon, 1996, p. 34). This Chapter starts with this postulation, but now, about hundred years later than William James, psychology has become a discipline with one of the highest numbers of students out of all study areas. Some students expect fascinating lectures about Freud's psychoanalysis, Jung's depth psychology and await such things as dream interpretation or how people can be seen through, and thus are rather surprised when they have to learn about perception, thinking, motivation and dry subjects such as statistics, data entry and mathematics. The discipline of psychology was only offered as an independent academic discipline from the end of the 19th century onwards. Prior to this, it was only mentioned as a side issue in subjects such as philosophy, medicine, pedagogy and theology. Particularly when it came to describing things that were not tangible, or rather were not measurable, then psychological terms or areas were partly taken up to cover this. No-one ever thought at that time that psychology would develop into an independent scientific discipline.

It is important to provide a definition of what psychology actually is, for then it can be demarcated from other disciplines. At the end of the 19th century, psychology was defined in Germany as "a science of the facts and laws of experience." The objects of research were the personal experiences of the individuals being questioned. These were to be researched into using scientific methods. However, this was queried by the American side and one of the questions that were debated was how could individual, emotional experience be scientifically investigated? (Krech & Crutchfeld, 1956) It was the behaviourists who began their work shortly before the First World War and described psychology as the "study of behaviour". Psychology was to limit itself to observable phenomena such as movements, words and glandular functions, which were to be studied with the help of objective methods.[1]

One can simply say that psychology is the science of the behaviour and experience of people. Dörner and Selg define psychology in the following way: The aims and purposes of psychology are to describe measure, explain and monitor human experience and behaviour, although monitor is meant here in terms of counselling or therapy (Dörner, Selg 1985).

The history of psychology shows that there can essentially be no standard definition of psychology, which is also due to the many currents within psychology itself. However, based on the literature reviewed, psychology can be defined as the description, measurement, explanation and monitoring of human behaviour. These are important areas in psychology.[2]

The following overview shows the main subject areas of psychology and their respective sub-sections and reveals how complex and varied psychology is. A psychology student looks into all these areas and later when qualified, specialises in one particular area. According to the APA (American Psychological Association) and the PASAR (Psychological Abstracts Search and Retrieval), psychology can be broken down as follows and shows the scope of this scientific discipline. Theoretical propaedeutic comprises statistics, methodology, psychophysics, scientific theory, psychopathology, philosophical and propaedeutic. This area concerns important introductory and basic areas of psychology which are normally taught at the beginning of the psychology course, in order to understand the origins, development and application of psychology. A further area of psychology is general psychology, which is concerned with the general areas of psychology. The emphasis here is the theoretical, conceptual and methodological area of the traditional subdisciplines in the area of psychology. To these belong neuropsychology, perceptual psychology, psychology of learning, activation psychology, cognitive psychology, emotion psychology. Differential psychology forms a further aspect of psychology. This area studies the ways in which individuals differ in their behaviour. This is distinguished from other aspects of psychology in that although psychology is ostensibly a study of individuals, modern

1 This will be detailed more extensively in the section "History of Psychology".
2 This will be detailed more extensively in the section "How do psychologists diagnose mental illness?".

psychologists often study groups or biological underpinnings of cognition. The sub-areas here are developmental psychology, personality psychology, psychodiagnostics, motivation psychology, social psychology and comparative psychology. Applied psychology forms the final significant aspect of psychology. Applied psychology describes psychological principles and theories to overcome problems in real life situations for human beings. Within this can be found clinical psychology, occupational psychology, industrial psychology, vocational psychology, traffic psychology, school psychology, environment psychology, advertising psychology and military psychology.

Although psychology did not exist as a university discipline until the beginning of the 20th century as compared to the other social science disciplines like theology, philosophy or medicine, it is still very complex and covers an incredibly large area. Some say that psychology has superseded subjects such as theology and philosophy or has overtaken them, and the fact that the number of mental illnesses worldwide is on the increase clearly shows how important psychology has become for humankind. It may be on the increase because psychology has become a recognisable discipline and that psychotherapy is recognised along with human experiences like depression, anxiety and trauma.

The academic requirements for studying psychology in Germany are extremely high and there are far more applicants than actual places. Psychology is the 'in thing' one could say. The number of popular scientific publications and of guides on diverse vital matters is also increasing and these are filling more and more the shelves in bookshops and libraries. However, the sheer scope of all the sections and sub-divisions of psychology also makes it clear that it is barely possible to have in-depth knowledge in every area. For this reason, many students choose to specialise in a specific area once their studies are completed.

In this thesis itself, it becomes clear that the subject matter of spirit possession is not purely placed within the field of psychology, but rather also reaches into the area of theology. The thesis will expound how spirit possession is categorised from the point of view of psychology, how this science deals with this phenomenon and which complex explanatory models exist etc. If the very same phenomenon and manifestation is described by a European researcher as a mental illness and by an African missionary as spirit possession, then the question must be asked as to whether both can be right?

1.1.1 What is the history of psychology?

The history of psychology began around the time of the early Greeks, although it was not until the late 1800's that it emerged as a discipline on its own (Boeree, 2006). The idea of dualism was introduced by the French philosopher René Descartes in the 17th century where it was claimed that human experience is formed by the interaction of the mind and body which are two separate entities. The philosophical traditions from these early days form the basis for many other topics which are discussed by psychologists in our day and age, for example the nature versus nurture debate and its relative contributions. In the past, philosophers used techniques involving observation and logic, whereas modern-day psychologists study and draw results concerning human thinking and behaviour patterns by employing scientific methods and principles (Hergenhahn, 2008).

Eventually psychology was acknowledged as a scientific discipline, aided along the way by physiology. Psychology was strongly influenced by research on the brain and studies of behaviour that were carried out by physiology in the past. This had an effect on the scientific methods and principles that were applied when researching human thinking and behaviour patterns. Wilhelm Wundt was a German physiologist who used such scientific research techniques to study reaction times in the middle of the 19th century. In 1874, he went on to write and publish a book called "Principles of Physiological Psychology" in which the important links between physiology and research into human thinking and behaviour patterns were detailed. It is thought that psychology was officially born as a separate scientific discipline when the first psychology laboratory in the world was started by Wundt at the University of Leipzig in 1879. He viewed psychology as the study of human consciousness and worked by using methods of experimentation in order to research into the inner processing of the mind.

Despite the fact that scientists now consider that Wundt's method of introspection cannot be relied upon and is no longer scientific, his research into psychology still cleared a way for the techniques of experimentation that are used today. His psychology lectures were attended by around 17,000 students, and hundreds more studied for psychology degrees and researched in his psychology laboratory. Although the impact of his studies lessened over time, it cannot be doubted how great his influence was upon the subject of psychology (Shiraev, 2011).

The first important school of thought in the area of psychology was set up by Edward B. Titchener who had studied under Wundt and went on to become one of his most famous students. It was claimed by the structuralists that it was possible to break human consciousness down into smaller parts. A method called introspection was employed where people who had received training tried to analyse their reactions and responses and break them down into fundamental awareness and feelings.

In America, psychology was growing, too, from the middle to the end of the 19th century. William James became known as the father of American psychology at this time after his book "The Principles of Psychology" was published. The latter became the most well-used textbook for psychology and out of James's ideas emerged functionalism, a new way of thinking, which concentrated on how behaviour aids people to live in their environment, using direct observation as one of its techniques. The human consciousness was significant in both structuralism and functionalism, but there were however major differences between the two approaches on how it was viewed. For the functionalists, consciousness was a process that never ceased and was always changing, whereas the structuralists' goal was to break down mental processes into smaller parts. Functionalism continued to have an influence on psychological approaches concerning thought processes and behaviour, although it no longer exists as its own school of thought. The techniques used by structuralism were based on scientific research, however these were not only subjective, but could also not be relied upon and had their limitations, too. The death of Titchener in 1927 also brought about the end of structuralism (Hergenhahn, 2011).

It was Sigmund Freud, a doctor from Austria, who brought about deep and significant changes to the discipline of psychology by emphasising how important the unconscious mind was. Freud worked in clinics with people who suffered from hysteria and various other persistent illnesses. His work here led him to the conclusion that the personality and behaviour of an adult is influenced by what the person experienced as a young child and by urges that originate in the unconscious mind. According to Freud, dreams express the thoughts and urges of the unconscious mind, as do "Freudian slips", i.e. slips of the tongue. His book "The Psychopathology of Everyday

Life" provides more details on these aspects, including his theory that when unconscious struggles are set off balance or become severe, then the outcome is a psychological illness. Freud's psychoanalytic approach not only had a very great influence in the area of psychology and on thinking in the 1900's, but also had an impact on other areas such as literature, popular culture and art. Although nowadays Freud has his sceptics, the depth of the impact he had on the area of psychology cannot be doubted.

At the beginning of the 1900's, a new approach called behaviourism became important and once more changed the face of psychology, making it again a more scientific discipline. The conscious and unconscious mind now played a much less significant role with this new school of thought concentrating on behaviour that could be observed. Ivan Pavlov, a Russian physiologist, was behaviourism's initiator with his studies on dogs' digestive systems. Through his research he discovered the process of classical conditioning showing that it was possible to learn behaviours through conditioned associations. He showed that it was possible to use the process of learning to draw an association between two stimuli, an environmental one and a naturally occurring one. In 1913, John B. Watson, an American psychologist, wrote about the basic principles of behaviourism in his paper "Psychology as the Behaviourist Views It", strongly advocating this approach to psychology. Watson explained in his book "Behaviourism" (Watson, 1924) that the subject matter of human psychology is the behaviour of the human being. It was his opinion that behaviourism claims that consciousness is neither a definite nor a usable concept. Watson described that the behaviourist, who has been trained as an experimentalist, maintains that belief in the existence of consciousness goes back to the ancient days of superstition and magic.

Behaviourism had a huge influence on psychology and held predominance for the next half a century. The theories of behaviourism were promoted by psychologist B.F. Skinner who showed how punishment and reinforcement affected behaviour, which he named operant conditioning. Although behaviourism's influence on psychology gradually ebbed away, its basic principles are still employed today. Children are helped to acquire new abilities and to surmount behaviours that are difficult to change with the use of therapeutic methods such as behaviour analysis, behavioural modification and token economies, and in upbringing and education, conditioning is also employed (O'Boyle, 2006).

In the late 1900's, a new approach, humanistic psychology, came to the fore, taking over from behaviourism and psychoanalysis which had both predominance in the early part of the century. Humanistic psychology placed the emphasis upon conscious experiences and became known as the "third force" in psychology. American psychologist Carl Rogers played an important role in founding this new approach. He emphasised the power of free will and self-determination, whereas the psychoanalyst studied unconscious urges and the behaviourist merely concentrated on environmental causes. Humanistic psychology was also promoted by the psychologist Abraham Maslow who drew up the well-known hierarchy of needs theory of human motivation.

The discipline of psychology has thus grown and changed greatly since its early days in the laboratory of Wilhelm Wundt, and since 1960 it has continued to develop with the introduction of further concepts and views. Many features of the human experience have been researched into by psychology over the last years, such as the influence of cultural and social factors and also how behaviour is affected by biological influences. Cognitive sciences, particularly brain research with all its possibilities, have also become a part of psychology in our day and age. Modern day psychologists tend to concentrate on a specialised area or view rather than working with a single approach, using concepts from various theories. New concepts and theories have emerged through the use of this varied approach and psychology will continue to evolve in future years.

It should be mentioned here that philosophy, and in particular religion, that is effectively theology, were the forerunners of psychology. Religion especially has influenced the view of the world and of people for over thousands of years, well before the epoch of science dawned. Thus it is natural, too, that all occurrences and phenomena that were unknown to man were explained using religious concepts of explanation and gods and powerful spirits were seen at work in for example natural catastrophes and in thunderstorms, too. For this reason, it was then a simple step for a belief in spirits to develop and some things which are attributed to psychic matters today were ascribed to spirits and demons in those days. Psychological experiences today were interpreted religiously in the past. This will appropriately be taken into account in this dissertation, for if a phenomenon of spirit possession in the past is attributed to a serious mental illness today (for example schizophrenia or a dissociative disorder), then it is clear that the whole topic concerns both areas of psychology and religion. For this reason, the first two chapters of this study are concerned with both subjects of psychology and theology. In particular the specialised topic of spirit possession is closely linked with both areas. For this reason, this study will examine the topic of spirit possession from the psychological as well as from the theological side. Firstly however, the fundamentals of mental illness will be discussed.

1.2 What is mental illness?

The American Psychiatric Association (APA) published the new Diagnostic and Statistic Manual of Mental Disorders (DSM-5) on 18th May 2013, as a follow-up to DSM-IV from 1994. In this publication mental illness or mental disorders are defined as follows: "A mental disorder is a syndrome characterized by clinically significant disturbance in an individual's cognition, emotion regulation, or behaviour that reflects a dysfunction in the psychological, biological, or developmental processes underlying mental functioning. Mental disorders are usually associated with significant distress in social, occupational, or other important activities. An expectable or culturally approved response to a common stressor or loss, such as the death of a loved one, is not a mental disorder. Socially deviant behaviour (e.g., political, religious, or sexual) and conflicts that are primarily between the individual and society are not mental disorders unless the deviance or conflict results from a dysfunction in the individual, as described above." (DSM-5, 2013). This definition of mental illness shows a broadening of the definition found in DSM-IV.

It cannot be consistently determined which mental illnesses occur most commonly, as can be seen in the following two examples from 2013, the first one from Germany and the second one from the USA. The statistics for Germany are more relevant for this study, but however statistics from the USA will be shown as a comparison. In 2013, the "Technische Universität" (University of Technology) in Dresden[3] questioned 5,318 German citizens between the ages of 18 and 79 about mental illnesses. 26.9% of those questioned claimed to be affected by a mental illness. 15.3% of these people suffered from anxiety

3 The TU Dresden is one of eleven German universities that were identified as an "excellence university". The TU Dresden is a multi-discipline university, also offering humanities and social sciences as well as medicine.

disorders, 7.9% from unipolar depression, 3.6% from obsessive-compulsive disorders and 1.5% suffered from bipolar disorders. Therefore, nearly a third of Germans suffer from a mental illness and these are the official figures, the number of unreported cases may well be higher than this. Since it is estimated that approximately a third of all Germans suffer from a mental disorder, this consequently has an effect on all areas of the German economy, for example concerning the number of sick days. The relative percentage of the incapacity for work due to mental illnesses is growing despite the declining rate of sick leave in recent years. It has increased in the past 39 years from two percent up to 14.7 percent. Sick days taken due to a mental illness have increased five-fold over this time period. Twenty years ago, mental illnesses were almost irrelevant, but today they are the second most common diagnosis for medical certificates for sick leave (BKK Health Report 2014). The consequence for companies and the national economy are expenses that run into billions; the direct sickness costs for mental illnesses on their own amount to just under 16 billion euros per year (Health and Safety Executive, 2011). According to this institute's calculations, they may rise to around 32 billion euros by the year 2030. What is more, the even larger percentage of indirect costs, caused by reduced productivity during the working years and premature retirement, is not even taken into account. The clear increase of sick days due to mental illness is reflected in the rising costs from loss of production. In 2008, it was estimated that these were just under four billion euros, but in 2012, the costs from loss of production had risen to six billion euros and they continue to increase. The same is true for the loss in the GVA (gross value added) due to sickness leave caused by mental illness; in the same period there was an increase here of more than three billion euros up to the amount of 10.5 billion euros (Federal Ministry of Labour and Social Affairs and Health and Safety Executive: "Safety and Health at Work" 2012, 2013).

The IGPP[4] in Freiburg, south Germany has been researching for decades into the area of paranormal phenomena and also has epidemiological data

4 The Institute for Frontier Areas of Psychology and Mental Health engages in systematic and interdisciplinary research concerning insufficiently understood phenomena and anomalies at the frontiers of current scientific knowledge. These include altered states of consciousness, exceptional human experiences, mind-matter relations, and their social, cultural and historical contexts from

available on the subject. National as well as international research results have been merging together for decades at the IGPP. There is transcultural evidence which shows that the number of people on an international level who believe in paranormal phenomena can be estimated at 60%–75%, and the number of those who have had their own experience of this is between 30%–50% (Newport & Strausberg, 2001; Schmied-Knittel & Schetsche, 2003). A sixth of Germans report having experienced a paranormal phenomenon at least once. Even if the phenomenon of spirit possession only represents a part of paranormal phenomena, this still shows that these things occur, and more often than is actually indicated on a worldwide basis as well as in Germany. These interpretations of spirit possession are not identical when compared internationally, details of which will be covered later in this study (cf. Chapter 1.4 Cultural expressions of mental illness).

A further study of the NAMI[5] determined that for the year 2013 every fourth American, approximately 61.5 million people, had something to do with mental illness and that approximately 20% of American young people between the ages of 13 and 18 suffered from a mental illness, and that for eight to13 year olds the number was 13%. 2.4 million Americans suffer from schizophrenia, that is 1.1% of all adults. 6.1 million Americans suffer from bipolar disorder, 14.8 million Americans suffer from a major depression and 42 million Americans suffer from anxiety disorders (National Institute of Health, Statistics 3, 2013).

A large percentage of psychologists, particularly in the western nations work with DSM-5 and ICD-10, but nevertheless mental illnesses are defined and explained in a different way in other parts of the world and in other cultures. Before the cultural differences in dealing with mental illnesses are detailed in this study, the following section will describe which general indications and possibilities exist in psychology at the moment for diagnosing mental illnesses.

---

the perspectives of the humanities, social sciences and natural sciences. http://www.igpp.de/english/welcome.htm.

5 NAMI is the National Alliance on Mental Illness, the "nation's largest grassroots mental health organization dedicated to building better lives for the millions of Americans affected by mental illness." NAMI advocates for access to services, treatment, supports and research and is steadfast in its commitment to raise awareness and build a community for hope for all of those in need. http://www.nami.org/template.cfm?section=About_NAMI.

1.3 How do psychologists diagnose mental illness?

Psychology has grown as a discipline from viewing mental illness as spirit possession to understanding it scientifically through various schools of thought. And now that these schools of thought dominate, what happens to those individuals who still experience, or believe that they have experienced, spirit possession? Are they misdiagnosed? Can there be collaboration between the discipline of psychology and the theories of theology? This thesis explains and gives answers.

In the field of medicine, equipment and somatic measuring systems are often used (for pulse/heartbeat, scales for weight, body-size, blood hypertension, blood pressure gauge for blood pressure, magnetic resonance imaging etc.) and psychologists also have various possibilities and tools which they use to diagnose mental illnesses in people who come to them seeking advice. Diagnosis is also very important in psychology, for it leads to the decision as to which further steps are to be taken concerning the psychological counselling and it is the prerequisite for an effective course of therapy. In addition to the personal impressions, speech and behaviour (mimic and gesture) of the person seeking advice, the following tools help to assess the person and his or her need and enable an exact diagnosis to be made.

1.3.1 General possibilities for diagnosis

- Questionnaires with questions about the life situation and the problems of the person seeking advice
- Questionnaires when certain disorders are suspected (addictive disorders, depression, sleeping problems, sexual disorders, communication problems…)
- Tests (personality test, intelligence tests, motivation tests, tests for particular mental disorders, e.g. for depression…)
- Specialist literature on diverse mental disorders and their therapies.
- Classification systems DSM-5 und ICD-10.

1.3.2 DSM-5 and ICD-10

DSM-5: The Diagnostic and Statistical Manual of Mental Disorders (DSM) is the standard classification of mental disorders used by mental health professionals in the United States and contains a listing of diagnostic criteria for every psychiatric disorder recognized by the U.S. healthcare system. The previous edition, DSM-IV, has been used by professionals in a wide array of contexts, including psychiatrists and other physicians, psychologists, social workers, nurses, occupational and rehabilitation therapists, and counselors, as well as by clinicians and researchers of many different orientations (e.g. biological, psychodynamic, cognitive, behavioural, interpersonal, family/systems). DSM is used in both clinical settings (inpatient, outpatient, partial hospital, consultation-liaison, clinic, private practice, and primary care) as well as with community populations. In addition to supplying detailed descriptions of diagnostic criteria, DSM is also a necessary tool for collecting and communicating accurate public health statistics about the diagnosis of psychiatric disorders (DSM-5, 2013).

ICD-10: The International Classification of Diseases (ICD) is the standard diagnostic tool for epidemiology, health management and clinical purposes. This includes the analysis of the general health situation of population groups. It is used to monitor the incidence and prevalence of diseases and other health problems, providing a picture of the general health situation of countries and populations (WHO, 2014). Chapter 5 deals with mental and behaviour disorders under notations F00 to F99. Here it should be pointed out that so-called "states of trance and possession" are listed in ICD-10 under Number F.44.3. Similar details are to be found in DSM-5 in the subsection 'Dissociative Disorders'.

1.3.3 Further indications for the diagnosis of mental illness

Psychologists therefore have a number of tools that can be used to recognise and diagnose mental illnesses. Ultimately these are aids to counselling and treating people more effectively. Each psychologist should be familiar with these tools, for the more he can utilise them, the better he is equipped for his work. A good diagnosis helps to classify specific mental symptoms. A good diagnosis on its own however is not enough to help. A therapy plan is needed which is individually drawn up for the person seeking advice. Or as the well-known German doctor, psychotherapist and theologian Manfred Lütz writes in his book *Irre, wir behandeln die Falschen* ("Crazy, we're treating the wrong ones"): "We know what diagnoses are, and especially what they are not. They are not truths but rather codewords which have the purpose of producing a suitable therapy" (Lütz, 2011, p. 83).

Even with the most precise diagnosis, the danger still exists of restricting people to a certain disorder, reducing them to their illness and effectively putting a stamp on them. Thus in some circumstances the disorder is seen more than the person who is suffering from the disorder. The person however is never the disorder, at the most he is suffering from one. For this reason, the social competences, the radiance and the communication skills are just as important for a successful therapy process as the diagnosed criteria. What additionally accounts for a large part of a successful treatment is the personality of the therapist and above all the patient-therapist-relationship. Much has been researched into here over recent years. In her thesis *Klient, Therapeut und das unbekannte Dritte* ("Client, therapist and the unknown third party" 2010), Nadine Reiband describes factors concerning the placebo effect which are taken less into consideration in psychotherapy. She comes to the conclusion that the placebo effect can only function in a purely medical model of psychotherapy and not in a contextual model. The medical model of psychotherapy is based on the assumption that certain contents which are based on concrete, characteristic theoretical suppositions, are the most important sources of psychotherapeutic effects. Proponents of this medical model predominantly believe in therapeutic effects which are brought about through specific intervention. The contextual model emphasises a holistic supposition in which general factors are very important, i.e. factors which also have a therapeutic effect and are *not* placebos (cf. Reiband, N., 2010, p. 15ff). The conclusion of her study is that special unspecific factors lead to positive therapeutic effects and thereby the therapeutic method and therapist adherence play a smaller role. A psychologist who wishes to give therapy should therefore, according to Reiband, take the following factors into account:

1.3.3.1 *The conviction of the psychologist towards the applied method*

If the therapist believes that a treatment is effective, then he or she will convey this belief enthusiastically to the client. This belief is meaningful for the clients (cf. ibid. p. 67).

1.3.3.2 *The therapist effect*

Within one method itself, the treatment results can vary considerably between different therapists. Reiband concludes that the therapist must be seen as a holistic factor (not just single individual therapist factors such as, among other things, subjectivity or objectivity, relatively stable personality traits, competence in method, philosophical orientation, rather the entirety). The essence of a therapy is embodied by the therapist, his conviction and his character traits. It depends on the therapist who applies the methods as to how successfully the therapy proceeds (cf. ibid. p. 81). The ignoring of the therapist effect in the study of psychotherapy led, according to Reiband's investigations, to an overestimation of the treatment effects which are brought about through method competence and therapist adherence. She points out that good treatment results here are possibly the result of a motivated and willing client (cf. ibid. p. 100) and thus due more to the client than to the therapist.

1.3.3.3 *Expectations of the client*

The expectations of the client that psychotherapy will be helpful and that they will be able to cope with matters which they could not cope with before, strengthens the client's morale and influences the results of the psychotherapy as a critical variable (cf. ibid. p. 86). Particularly the positive expectations *before* the treatment showed a correlation to the actual improvement *during* the treatment.

1.3.3.4 *Feedback*

Regular feedback from the client to the therapist is of significant importance. Feedback makes clear as to where steady improvement is missing and helps to identify incorrect treatment in time. Thus the amount of times that treatment is terminated can be reduced and the client is personally kept informed of important information about the success or failure of the therapy (cf. ibid. p. 93).

1.3.3.5 Medication

Finally, the whole area of medication is important with the issue of mental illness. In Germany, psychiatrists who have a medical background from their training often work with anti-depressants, neuroleptics and tranquilisers and this in turn is criticised by many psychologists. The latter view medication more as a support for psychotherapy and criticise the psychiatrists for using these types of medication as a panacea. An integrative procedure is effectively called for here, with less "either ... or" and with more of both sides.

To conclude, it can be said that the diagnostic instruments as well as the medication are very helpful, but not as a panacea. Every form of diagnosis which concerns the classical counsellor qualifications such as empathy, appreciation, the valuing of each individual personality and the ability to communicate effectively should be enhanced. The therapist-client-relationship should be taken into account in order to ensure the most effective therapy for mental illnesses.

There is therefore a multitude of diagnosis possibilities in the area of psychology which can be employed. When it is specifically about the subject of spirit possession, then the tools described above are used from the psychological side in order to work out a diagnosis. There are experts who postulate trance and possession phenomena. The next section will show that these tools are not handled in the same way everywhere and are not available in the same measure everywhere either, for the world is not only made up of the western industrial nations, but of other continents, too, and it will become clear that the cultural background of those seeking advice and of those who provide help can not only be very varied, but should also be taken into consideration in every case.

1.4 Cultural expressions of mental illness

The social practices, as well as the religious-traditional conditions of the respective countries, play a significant role. Results are different in parts of the world which have a solid foundation of piety and over centuries of traditional beliefs (e.g. in Africa, South America and Asia) compared to the communist or socialist regions of the world. Thus in the western world, for example, mental illnesses are diagnosed much more often than in other parts of the world. In the industrialised nations, considerably more psychiatric institutions are to be found than in other continents and the same applies for the administering of psychotropic drugs. Albert C. Gaw (Gaw, 1993) shows results from his three years research work together with 33 colleagues who made it their task to establish the connection between culture and mental illness worldwide. Here it is described that the psychotherapeutic work is significantly influenced by the cultural surroundings, regardless of where in the world. What applies on a large scale also applies on a small scale, i.e. that it is important in the psychotherapeutic setting to enquire about the cultural background of the patient. In this day and age with such a flow of refugees and immigration this is vital. Also the understanding in the area of speech is essential since the basis for every therapeutic process must be that the therapist and the patient meet on the same language level. In the book by Gaw specific questions are provided as to how one can explore the cultural background of the person seeking advice. This is important because the culture defines what is allowed and what is forbidden, what is normal and what is not normal. Thus it is not surprising that in one culture the "hearing of voices" counts as a religiously-cultural normal occurrence, while in another culture schizophrenia would be spoken of. Both positions have different consequences so that one person is "revered" and the other, in the worst possible case, is admitted to the psychiatric unit of the mental hospital. But also how people deal with time, eating behaviour, sexuality, the meaning of looks etc. varies from culture to culture. If it is then also taken into account that the diverse beliefs are different, it becomes clear that there can be no consistent understanding of mental illness and that there doesn't need to be one either. Obviously cultures also have an influence on people's cognitive systems, which means that thinking is also subject to the cultural norms. This has an enormous influence on therapeutic practice especially where cognitive approaches are concerned. The social-communicative side should likewise be thoroughly taken into account. Since identity is lived out in groups in various cultures, while elsewhere the autonomous identity has priority, so will this social behaviour also have an influence on the course of therapy. "Perspectives of Clinical Parapsychology", published in 2012, is a compilation of results from a conference in the Netherlands in 2007, where 20 experts from eight different countries met together. Here they compared the reports they had brought with them from people who had experienced various paranormal phenomena, including states of spirit possession. These experts also compiled their results and these made it clear that it is imperative to take the cultural aspect into account. The same phenomena can be interpreted in different ways according to the background and then can also be treated differently according to this.

In Europe, the subject of possession is also dealt with in different ways and the religious traditions constitute an essential factor as well. In countries with a solid foundation of piety (e.g. Italy and Poland, both influenced and shaped by Catholicism) demon possession is dealt with in a different way than in other countries. Science is also researching into this area.

Whether in different continents or in connection with the topic of immigration and refugees, psychologists and therapists should not underestimate the cultural effect here.

1.5 Spirit possession from a psychological perspective

Psychology does not assume the existence of a devil, demons etc. as theology does, but rather attempts to classify these phenomena in a different way. Some national and international scientists do accept terms such as trance and the condition of possession, however they contextualise and explain these terms differently to theologians. Later there follows some current approaches and explanatory models, or interpretations of spirit possession from a psychological point of view, by scientists and institutes who have been carrying out research in this subject matter for years. After examining the relevant psychological teaching books including DSM-5 and ICD-10 and looking at the international state of research and then focusing on Germany, it soon becomes clear that there are no unified positions with regard to the international research results. The social practices, as well as the religious-traditional conditions of the respective countries, play a significant role. Results are different in parts of the world which have a solid foundation of piety and over centuries of traditional beliefs (e.g. in Africa, South America and Asia) compared to the communist or socialist regions of the world. The Transcultural Psychiatry has investigated these socio-cultural circumstances with regard to possession psychoses and for example describes the fact that in Latin America, Africa and South East

Asia incantational prayers, authoritarian-suggestive therapy methods and liturgical rites, bordering on magic, are a regular feature of healing for people who consider themselves possessed. In other parts of the world this is less or never the case. The belief in some cultures that a person can be possessed is spread worldwide and when literature is examined on this subject, four explanatory models come up again and again showing what demon possession could be.

Samuel Pfeiffer, who has conducted various studies on this (Pfeiffer, 1999), summarises the explanatory models as follows:

1.5.1 Culture-bound phenomenon

Possession states are seen as a culturally-accepted phenomenon. Possession is not necessarily an illness, but rather a process which is deliberately induced as part of healing rituals.

1.5.2 Witchcraft explanations

Mental illness is acknowledged as such, but is interpreted as the consequence of magical rituals or witchcraft, resulting in emotional suffering and culturally abnormal behaviour.

1.5.3 Hysteria and dissociation

This early psychopathological interpretation of possession is to be found in psychoanalytic theory which has interpreted possession as a form of culturally shaped hysteria. Over the last 20 years there seems to be a paradigm shift in psychiatric theory relevant to spirit possession toward the concept of dissociation, which has been described as Dissociative Identity Disorder.

1.5.4 Delusions

A Japanese study (Iida, 1989) found that 21% of 1029 inpatients had a delusion of possession. Most of them were under 30 years of age and diagnosed with schizophrenia. In a US study of 61 chronically psychotic outpatients the authors found a delusion of possession in 25 subjects. The comparison of these 25 possessed patients with 36 patients without a history of delusional possession revealed significantly more reports of childhood sexual abuse, higher dissociation scores, more cannabis abuse, more experience of thought control, and more voices heard inside their heads.

Samuel Pfeiffer also conducted a systematic investigation of the prevalence of this attribution in 343 mainly Protestant out-patients of a psychiatric clinic in Switzerland, who described themselves as religious. 129 (37.6%) of these believed in the possible causation of their problems through the influence of evil spirits, labelling this as occult bondage or possession.

Johannes Mischo's research (Mischo, 1985) is about "An interdisciplinary approach to the question of demonic possession". He points out four perspectives that are relevant to an interdisciplinary discussion of demonic possession. From anthropological investigations of 700 primitive cultures distributed all over the world, common patterns of possession are drawn and natural explanations are confronted with the supernatural ones that are current in the respective countries of origin.

Special attention should be paid on the practice of exorcism carried out by the Roman Catholic Church; this has been modified over the 2000 years of church history and is now promoted by the current Pope. To this very day exorcism remains a feature of Catholic teaching and liturgy. A difference is made between *simple exorcism* and *major or solemn exorcism.* For example the baptism rite contains a simple exorcism, since the baptizand is freed from original sin and its instigator; the devil, and also renounces the latter (or rather the godparents do this in his or her stead). The carrying out of a solemn exorcism is reserved for a a priest only and requires the special permission of the bishop. The rite is regulated in the newly revised section of the "Rituale Romanum" *De exorcismis et supplicationibus quibusdam* from 1999. The solemn exorcism, according to the *Catechism of the Catholic Church (CCC),* serves to "expel demons or liberate from demonic possession using the power of spiritual authority which Jesus entrusted to his Church" (CCC no. 1673). A difference is clearly made between mental illnesses and the state of demon possession. Mental illnesses are a matter for the doctors. Before a solemn exorcism is carried out, the church must be certain that this is really a case of possession and not mental illness. It is imperative that one or more expert opinions from independent doctors and psychologists are sought. The ritual dates back to 1614, but 385 years later in 1999 it was revised by the Congregation for Divine Worship and the Discipline of the Sacraments and strict requirements were added. The approach of Spirit Releasement Therapy, also seen as a modern version of the "Rituale Romanum", was developed by William and Judith Baldwin (Baldwin, 1991). It is not really taken seriously in academic circles, but should be mentioned here for the sake of completeness. SRT attempts to do a balancing act between theological and therapeutic approaches and in doing so falls short in every instance. The situation is similar with the approach of Remote Depossession, by Irene Hackmann, a friend of the Baldwin couple. Both approaches are on offer in the USA for a price of 300 US dollars upwards. At this point reference should be made to three current scientific publications which were published in 2012:

"Veränderte Bewusstseinszustände" (Altered States of Consciousness), by Dieter Vaitl, the director of BION (Bender Institute of Neuroimaging). The studies he used as a basis (Bourguignon, 1968, Blackmore, 2007) are ones which have researched altered states of consciousness in cultures worldwide from the 1970's up to today. In his book he is concerned with explaining the connection between the results of current brain research and altered states of consciousness in people.

"Exorzismus oder Therapie" (Niemann, 2005) (Exorcism or Therapy) is a classic on this subject (though already out of print). The author describes the tension between the theological and psychological approach to the subject of demon possession. In the chapter "Verrückt oder besessen?" (Crazy or possessed?) the author explains that with the diagnosis for people who felt they were overwhelmed and influenced by evil, various individual-genetic, biographical, somatic, psychodynamic and socio-cultural areas were explored (ibid. p. 111)

Also a standard work with a psychotherapeutic background is the book "Außergewöhnliche Erfahrungen" (Belz, 2009) (Exceptional Experiences'. Martina Belz from the University of Zurich (Switzerland) describes the current position on the phenomenology of exceptional experiences and presents psychophysical explanatory models (synchronicity theory, generalised quantum theory, model of pragmatic information). Furthermore, the book discusses diagnostic and therapeutic strategies as to how those seeking advice can be specifically helped and assigns possession to the "spectrum disorder of internal presence". Here it is predominantly concerned with auditive and somatic phenomena. This internal presence is often described as a takeover of one's own body from the outside. Conventional attempts at explaining this say that those affected are pantopragmatics or liars and that their experiences are based on delusion. Moreover, conspiracy theories are depicted or in extreme cases the affected person is said to be bedeviled or accursed. Long distance hypnosis, voodoo magic, demonisation or demonic possession are likewise given as a reason for the appearance of an internal presence. From the scientific approach it is often postulated that a person fails to recognise reality. He or she is hallucinating, possibly as a result of derealisation – or from having episodes of dissociation. Dissociative processes take place. Delirium, psychoses or extreme mourning sorrow can lead to the hearing of voices (Belz, 2009).

Emma Cohen, Professor at the University of Oxford, who teaches at the Institute of Cognitive and Evolutionary Anthropology describes recurrent features of spirit possession in her article *What is Spirit Possession? Defining, Comparing, and Explaining, Two Possession Forms.* She discovered that the concept of spirit possession falls into two forms: One that entails the transformation or replacement of identity (executive possession) and one that envisages possessing spirits as illness and misfortune (pathogenetic possession). In her article she draws from the famous work by Erika Bourguignon, one of the most popular anthropological scholars of spirit possession. Bourguignon published a book entitled Possession, in which she presented a cross-cultural analysis of possession beliefs and behaviours. Bourguignon and Emma Cohen speak about two forms of possession. Both possession forms entail the direct actions of spirit entities in or on a person's body. Cohen's opinion is that pathogenetic possession concepts result from the operation of cognitive tools that deal with the representation of contamination (both positive and negative). She postulates that the presence of the spirit entity is typically (but not always) manifested in the form of illness. Executive possession concepts mobilise cognitive tools that deal with the world of intentional agents; the spirit entity is typically represented as taking over the host's executive control, or replacing the host's mind (or intentional agency), thus assuming control of bodily behaviours.

1.6 Interdisciplinary approach to spirit possession

The topic of spirit possession essentially reaches into the areas of theology and psychology, as mentioned several times already. The theological/historical perspective shows vital ways of how the course has been set for the diagnosis of possession and its therapy, starting from the exorcism methods of the early church up to today's theories and practices (cf. Chapter 2). The psychological perspective predominantly assumes the appearance of dissociative identity disorders and for these suggests treatment techniques and medication. Johannes Mischo, who has already been mentioned, worked out common patterns concerning the topic of spirit possession, based on anthropological investigations of 700 primitive cultures distributed all over the world. He proposes four perspectives which are to be considered against a scientific background.

1.6.1 The Anthropological Perspective

At the beginning of the 1960's, a study on the transcultural investigation of dissociative conditions in 700 primitive cultures was carried out worldwide by the Ohio State University. In the process, the Judaeo-Christian area was deliberately excluded and so it dealt with non-Christian cultures in Africa, the Caribbean, Islamic countries, India and North Asia. Erika Bourguignon published these results in her classic "World distribution and patterns of possession states" (Bourguignon, 1968). The study revealed that dissociative conditions, and thus also the area of spirit possession, primarily only permit two explanatory models: Natural or supernatural. Both models are found in these cultures. Interestingly both are also found in more highly developed cultures.

1.6.1.1 Natural explanations

Here hypnosis, dissociation, fear, somatic and psychosomatic illnesses are assumed. Sicknesses such as dissociative identity disorder (previously known as multiple personality disorder), hysteria, psychosis, epilepsy and febrile states are diagnosed.

The study revealed that in the area of supernatural explanations, two areas are indicated: Trance possession and spirit possession without trance.

1.6.1.2 Trance possession

Here it is assumed that external powers have invaded a person; these can be evil spirits or an impersonal influence.

1.6.1.3 Spirit possession without trance

Here the possession is interpreted as powers having invaded a person which then cause a condition of illness. In many cases witchcraft and bedevilment are assumed.

1.6.2 The theological/historical perspective

Chapter 2.3 (Theological history of spirit possession) provides more details on this perspective.

1.6.3 The social-psychological perspective of Protestant and Catholic theologians

Johannes Mischo refers here to the survey "Fragen über den Teufel" (Questions about the devil) carried out among theologians of the Roman Catholic as well as of the Protestant Church (Hammers und Rosin, 1974). The results of this representative survey show that Protestant theologians distance themselves considerably more from a personal form of evil than the Catholics do. Although up to two thirds of the Catholic theologians accept the tradition that has been passed on, they still prefer to turn to psychologists in specific counselling situations rather than to their own exorcists. This difference between theory and practice challenges above all the Catholic theologians to develop new statements of opinion which are suitable for reducing this discordance (Mischo, 1985).

1.6.4 The medical-psychological perspective

The spirit possession researcher, Oesterreich, who also carried out many intercultural investigations in this area, reaches the conclusion that with a case of spirit possession, the whole behaviour of expression of a person changes considerably. The way the voice speaks changes, as well as the content of the words spoken. A new ego emerges that leads a form of its own life alongside the "normal" ego. Oesterreich assumes that it is a case of the appearance of so-called multiple personalities following a split in personality. Previously this was placed in its own category in the DSM-III as Multiple Personality Disorder (MPD). Today it is found under the rubric of "Dissociative Identity Disorder" in the new DSM-5.

When classifying the topic of spirit possession against a psychological background there is therefore relatively generous room for manoeuvre. Against the current background this understanding reaches barely, if at all, into that of theology, particularly when personal, evil and demonic powers are spoken about. The second chapter of this study will show how this is also not consistently portrayed in the field of theology. And thus the difficulties for free church pastors become increasingly clear.

2 Theology and Spirit Possession

Chapter 2 mentioned the definitions of the terms theology and spirit procession, also the historic development of the term spirit possession in theological Context. Hereafter it is shown how the pastors are trying to ascertain the spirit possession, respectively to diagnose it and how especially difficult it is for these professional groups to put this proceeding in practice. As a thematic completion follows the theological-biblical perspective about spirit possession in Old and New Testament at the end of the chapter.

2.1 What is Theology?

Theology is a word from the Greek language (qeos and logos) and means the words or the teaching of or about God and describes the teachings and contents of, in this case, the Christian religion. Since Christianity is a book religion, like Islam and Judaism, too, Christian theology is thus based on the texts of the Bible, that is on the Old and New Testaments and what has been said about them in the course of over 2000 years of church history. Similar to psychology, theology also has various sub-disciplines. These include church history, dogmatic (different Christian teachings), exegesis (interpretation of biblical texts), homiletics (learning to preach) and practical theology (for example weddings, funerals, communion). The sub-discipline of angelology, that is to say the teaching about angels, can be found in the area of dogmatic. Here the subject of demons is also dealt with.

Theology overlaps with psychology at this point, since pastors believe in the existence of demons/spirits on the basis of their theological education, but in a counselling situation they do not have the necessary psychological knowledge to enable them to differentiate between, for example, a demonic burden (theology) and schizophrenia, personality disorder, or catatonic states or delusions (psychology). The need to differentiate and understand the distinction or overlap between demonic and psychological experiences, is needless to say, imperative. The urgency rests with the need to be able to appropriately treat individuals with the relevant intervention.

Christianity, which developed out of Judaism and sees Jesus of Nazareth as its founder and key figure, began its triumphal march at Pentecost. The latter is seen as the day the church of Jesus Christ was born and since then Christianity has spread out across the whole world and is considered to be the most widespread religion on the earth. The Bible is likewise the most widespread book in the world. The overlap of psychological experiences and belief in possession demands an elaboration on the belief systems that advocates the existence of spirit possession.

Christian theology is, despite the above-stated teaching disciplines, not unified and thus each church is never exactly the same in its conventions. The two largest lines of Christianity are the Roman Catholic Church and the Protestant Church. To some extent there are considerable differences between these two churches, historically as well as doctrinally. Opinions are deeply divided over issues such as Bible understanding, veneration of Mary and the saints, communion or the Papacy. In Germany, there are therefore explicitly Catholic and Protestant church congresses. There have just been two ecumenical congresses in Germany up to now, in Berlin in 2003and in Munich in 2010.

A wide spectrum of church landscapes is to be found on the continents of the earth, depending on the country and its social anthropology. As well as the Catholic and Protestant churches, a further line has developed over the last centuries, namely that of the free churches. These are widespread and also differ from each other, though the common features of their theological principles are basically the same. These are the evangelical fundamentals: the Bible as God's word, the necessity of being born again, Jesus as the only way to God, heaven and hell after death, the return of Jesus. Since the 20th century a young Christian movement has become more and more well-known: the Pentecostal-Charismatic movement. This is characterised by its liveliness and supernatural elements such as healings, speaking in tongues and prophecies. The expelling of demons is also practiced; here it is called deliverance ministry, but is similar to the exorcism of the Catholic Church, even though it is handled in a very different way. It is precisely the varying theological concepts concerning spirit possession which explain why churches and their pastors deal with this phenomenon in different ways. These issues will be examined more closely in the following section.

2.2 What is spirit possession?

Since early times there has been a fascination with spirit possession that finds expression through human bodies. The afflicted individual is believed to have a spirit enter his or her body, taking control over their mind, body and behaviour. The consequence of such an experience results in behaviour that can be described as anti-social, violent, disruptive, strange and bizarre and, simply put, scary, to those who interact or come into contact with the possessed. Spirit possession can be defined as the inner seizing of occupation of a person by an external personality, a god, a spirit or another power, where this person's independence is to a large extent or totally deactivated (Daxelmüller, 1979). As well as artificially induced and ceremonial possession, for example in possession-shamanism, there is also spontaneous, involuntary possession, in particular where demon possession by demonic spiritual beings plays a role. It is differentiated from "Umsessenheit", which is when demonic beings come from the outside and lurk around and harass the person concerned (Daxelmüller, 1979).

Spirit or demonic possession is found in nearly every culture and can be described as the "mental and motor take-over of a human personality" (Rogo, 1974, p. 18). The phenomenon of possession appears in practically the same way across diverse cultures, in fact when the history, culture and archaeology across different civilisations is studied, it is found that these nearly all support a concept of supernatural beings (Cevendish, 1967; Prins, 1992). Although other religions recognise the existence of demon possession, it is only Christianity which postulates that one can be possessed by an entirely evil diabolical enemy. Islam holds that people, usually women, can be possessed by 'djinns' and 'zar spirits' which bring about illness, defiance and disharmony within the marriage (Guiley, 1992). Hinduism also has a widespread belief in spirit possession and women in particular often hold evil spirits responsible for such things as miscarriage and infertility, period pains, domestic violence and adultery (Guiley, 1992). It seems that most religious belief systems include the belief in spirit possession. As the Christian religion spread across Europe and slowly trickled onto other continents, so did the belief in spirit possession. Well into the 1800's, a person with a mental illness was thought to be demon possessed, despite the fact that medical circles generally acknowledged hysteria to be a natural condition (Spanos & Gottlieb, 1979). In fact, the history of psychology itself points to the treatment of hysteria as a form of possession (Spanos & Gottlieb, 1979).

But possession is complex and in order to understand it, we need to explore the types of possession that are acknowledged. There are two main forms of demon possession: Obsession or lucid possession and trance or somnambulistic possession (Ellenberger, 1970; Crabtree, 1985).

Obsession or lucid possession:

In the first form of possession, the person is influenced by demons to such an extent that they become unwillingly obsessed in their mind and imagination with "unclean, evil or sinful" preoccupations. These three words must be viewed from within a Christian ideological framework, since "unclean, evil and sinful" preoccupation reflects behaviour that is against the will of the Christian God.

Trance or somnambulistic possession:

The second form of possession, trance and somnambulistic possession, is a more acute form of demonization where demons occupy a person's mind and body to the extent where they take total control over that person (Cavendish, 1975; Ellenberger, 1970; Prins, 1992; Robins, 1959). In this type of possession, the person is no longer conscious of self and talks in the personality of the 'demon'. For the Catholic Church, a genuine possession is a trance possession. Both types of possession can be seen as "a kind of psychic parasitism: just as a tapeworm can live in the body, so can a parasitic spirit live in the soul" (Ellenberger, 1970, p. 13).

According to Crabtree (1985) there are three types of entities that can possess an individual:

- Firstly, there are 'supernatural personal entities' which exist independently in their own right.
- Secondly, 'non-personal entities' which do not have independent minds, are the creation of other minds and exist by energy.
- Thirdly, 'intrapsychic entities' which invade the conscious self but are unconscious parts within the personality.

Having elaborated on what is characteristic of spirit possession, the following section provides a theological understanding of the experience.

2.3 Theological history of spirit possession

Below an overview will be given as to how the theological understanding of spirit possession has developed over the millennia. It will become clear that the theological term of possession can never be rigidly defined, rather has always been a 'child of its times' and remains so today. The understanding that people can be possessed by demons is already mentioned in early cultures and epochs of human history, for example in the Gilgamesch-Epos (Nugent, 1987). The belief in the existence of non-human personal beings was repeatedly made responsible for the evil in the world. But even when the devil or a demon is spoken of as a person, there is still no comprehensive and conclusive definition of evil provided. Evil is ultimately an incomprehensible phenomenon and remains inconceivable and unexplainable from its very origin (Niemann, 2005). How theology has handled the phenomenon of spirit possession over the last two millennia will now be explained.

2.3.1 Antiquity, the Bible and early Christianity

As early as Greek mythology and tragedy, insanity was sent by the gods. In the world view from antiquity, demons were self-evident and Plato (427–347 BC) in particular and his philosophy made this clear. The belief in demons and spirits in antiquity was not statistical but rather developed over the course of time. In early Greece, demons were not only seen as negative, but essentially were seen as non-material, transcendent beings. Very early on, the term of 'daemon' described God himself, later his attendants (for example the satyrs of Dionysus). Later, intermediate beings between God and man were described as this and finally demons were a spiritual being that belonged to a particular person (for example Agathodaemon, the guardian spirit of Socrates). Later still, with Aeschylus or Euripides the spiritual beings of deceased demons were named. In the course of Judaism and Christianity, the belief in demons and spirits was interpreted as negative due to biblical statements. (Osjord-Naegeli, 2007, p. 48–50).

In Jewish monotheism there are few indications, according to the Old Testament, of a distinct belief in demons. Satan as a heavenly being and his fall suggest an initial development leading to a belief in demons. In the first book of Chronicles, the devil is linked to the archetype of evil, but as a rule however in the Old Testament the individual person is made responsible for evil behaviour. The background to this is the fall of man through Adam and Eve which is described in Genesis, chapter 3. The story of the fall of man in the Garden of Eden is a feature of all monotheistic religions (Judaism, Christianity, Islam). In this they see not only the fall of man away from God, but also the distance between the creator and the created and finally dualism develops out of this for all these religions – the battle between good and evil, between God and the devil, between light and darkness.

When the people of Israel in the Old Testament were taken into imprisonment in Babylon from 587–538 BC, the distance between God and his people increased considerably and became more accentuated. It was exactly this area, between God and man, between creator and the created, which was now increasingly filled with all sorts of angels, spirits and sons of God. The result of this was that the originally multi-layered concept of God was relieved from seemingly contradictory characteristics. Where evil comes from, when ultimately everything originates from God, was resolved in this way: Satan, who was originally a good angel rose up against God and thus from his own free will turned away from God. In the New Testament the devil, Satan, Lucifer was then God's opponent and all things, including the demons, are subordinate to him. Demons, as harmful spirits and in particular as demons of illness, became the subject of the healings and exorcisms that Jesus and his disciples carried out.[6] In his book 'Old Jewish Demonology', Billerbeck describes the beliefs of late Judaism about Satan and demons. Every sin and passion was assigned to a demon and demons were also the cause of illnesses. The origin of demons as servants of Satan was ascribed to the spirits or souls of deceased giants. These giants had come into being when the fallen angels had had union with human women (Genesis 6:1–4). The earth, air, houses, fields, deserts, ruins, watering holes and certain bushes and trees were adopted by demons as dwelling places. The main time when the demons were active was at night, occasionally demonic activity in the morning and afternoon were also mentioned, according to Billerbeck.

6 This will be detailed more extensively in the section "Theological Theories of Spirit Possession".

2.3.2 The Middle Ages and Exorcism in the Catholic Church

During the Middle Ages, spirit possession was understood as "the dwelling of a demon inside a human body". The soul of the person remained untouched, since this ruled over the body, according to the belief of those days (Jehl, 2005). The driving out of demons also served the Church as an indication of its own legitimisation and of its direct access to God as the highest authority of all benedictive and supernatural powers. Due to the emerging competition from newly formed Protestantism, the Roman Catholic Church tried to prove through more and more spectacular exorcisms that it was the better and only true Church. Thus in the 16th to 17th centuries, public driving out of demons and witch-hunts were carried out. Exorcism has a long tradition, mainly in the Roman Catholic Church, but its history is far longer and therefore older than that of Catholic teaching and liturgy. A difference is made between *simple exorcism* and *major or solemn exorcism.* For example, the baptism rite contains a simple exorcism, since the candidate is freed from original sin and its instigator the devil and also renounces the latter (or rather the godparents do this in his or her stead). The solemn exorcism was carried out among others by Pope Leo XIII and includes calling to the archangel Michael, a saying to break a curse, reading of Psalm 68/67, a new saying to break a curse, as well as the final prayer. The carrying out of a solemn exorcism is reserved for a priest only and requires the special permission of the bishop. The rite is regulated in the newly revised section of the "Rituale Romanum" *De exorcismis et supplicationibus quibusdam* from 1999. The solemn exorcism, according to the *Catechism of the Catholic Church (CCC),* serves to "expel demons or liberate from demonic possession using the power of spiritual authority which Jesus entrusted to his Church" (CCC no. 1673). A difference is clearly made between mental illnesses and the state of demon possession. The Roman Catholic Church is clear on this point: Mental illnesses are a matter for the doctors. Before a solemn exorcism is carried out, the church must be certain that this really is a case of possession and not mental illness. It is imperative that one or more expert opinions from independent doctors and psychologists are sought. The "Rituale Romanum" dates back to 1614, but 385 years later in 1999, it was revised by the Congregation for Divine Worship and the Discipline of the Sacraments and strict requirements were added. There follow some extracts on exorcism from the Codex Iuris Canonici 1172:

§1: No one can perform exorcisms legitimately upon the possessed unless he has obtained special and express permission from the local ordinary.

This passage makes it clear how important it was for the Catholic Church to have exorcism embedded in the church structures and that it could only be carried out by someone who had authorisation from the governing body of the church.

§2: The local ordinary is to give this permission only to a presbyter who has piety, knowledge, prudence, and integrity of life.

As well as church permission and authorisation, importance was placed on the skills and the personal qualities of the priest. Integrity and truthfulness were inseparably linked to the ministry of exorcism. Spiritual authority was connected to a holy life style.

Chapter 517: Christ's whole life is a mystery of redemption. Redemption comes to us above all through his blood spilled on the cross (cf. Ephesians 1:7; Colossians 1:13–14; 1 Peter 1:18–19) but this mystery is at work throughout Christ's entire life: Already in his incarnation through which by becoming poor he enriches us with his poverty (cf. 2 Corinthians 8:9); in his hidden life which by his submission atones for our disobedience (cf. Luke 2:51); in his word which purifies its hearers (cf. John 15:3); in his healings and exorcisms by which "he took our infirmities and bore our diseases" (Matthew 8:17) (cf. Isaiah 53:4); and in his resurrection by which he justifies us (cf. Romans 4:25).

These statements were used to justify the theological legitimacy of exorcism. It must come from the Holy Scripture and be found in the paragon and head of the church, Jesus of Nazareth. Based on the encompassing salvation through Jesus, from guilt and sin as well as from illness and pain, and the victory over all powers of darkness, one can assume that, through exorcism, God will help those who are possessed.

Chapter 550: The coming of God's kingdom means the defeat of Satan's (cf. Matthew 12:36): "If it is by the Spirit of God that I cast out demons, then the kingdom of God has come upon you" (Matthew 12:28). Jesus' exorcisms free some individuals from the domination of demons (cf. Luke 8:26–39). They anticipate Jesus' great victory over "the ruler of this world" (John 12:31). The kingdom of God will be definitively established through Christ's cross: "God reigned from the wood" (LH, Hymnus "Vexilla Regis").

The coming of the kingdom of God, in the sign of exorcism, too, was considered as confirmation of this ministry. The Catholic Church saw itself as commissioned by Jesus and where demons were driven out, there Jesus' power and strength were made clear and God's kingdom became visible.

Chapter 1237: Since Baptism signifies liberation from sin and from its instigator the devil, one or more exorcisms are pronounced over the candidate. The celebrant then anoints him with the oil of catechumens, or lays his hands on him, and he explicitly renounces Satan. Thus prepared, he is able to confess the faith of the Church, to which he will be "entrusted" by Baptism (cf. Romans 6:17).

Baptism as one of the sacraments of the Roman Catholic Church conveys the fact that the one baptised is crucified, dies and is buried with Christ. According to Romans chapter 6 Christians are to be God's servants and no longer slaves to sin and the devil. Whoever has been baptised, has this new life and the old, evil, demonic has gone.

Chapter 1673: When the Church asks publicly and authoritatively in the name of Jesus Christ that a person or object be protected against the power of the Evil One and withdrawn from his dominion, it is called exorcism. Jesus performed exorcisms (cf. Mark 1:25–26) and from him the Church has received the power and office of exorcising (cf. Mark 3:15; 6, 7:13; 16:17). In a simple form, exorcism is performed at the celebration of Baptism. The solemn exorcism, called "a major exorcism," can be performed only by a priest and with the permission of the bishop. The priest must proceed with prudence, strictly observing the rules established by the Church. Exorcism is directed at the expulsion of demons or to the liberation from demonic possession through the spiritual authority which Jesus entrusted to his Church. Illness, especially psychological illness, is a very different matter; treating this is the concern of medical science. Therefore, before an exorcism is performed, it is important to ascertain that one is dealing with the presence of the Evil One, and not an illness (cf. CIC, can. 1172).

Here it is made clear that possession is not a mental illness but is rather attributed to the direct influence of Satan and his demons. A distinction was made between illness and possession. The Church therefore tried to deal responsibly with those seeking advice as well as with the specific practice of exorcism.

The Church rituals in this area at first differed, but were then standardised in the Rituale Romanum of 1614. At that time, a feature of spirit possession was believed to be when the person affected spoke in an unknown language, declared things which he could not know about, and exhibited a physical power which extended above and beyond his age and condition. There were also many characteristics in those days which indicated a case of spirit possession: a bent body, immobility, remaining silent, yelling, and swearing. Those affected were from every social class and even the clergy were not excluded from the possibility of having possessed people in their own ranks. Overall more women were affected than men and most of them had the wish to be set free from the evil powers which plagued them (De Waardt, 2005). As early as in this first significant rule (Rituale Romanum) it was to be differentiated between spirit possession or suffering from black bile, melancholy or another illness, since a demonic influence could only be accepted if there was no natural explanation for it. This was a change compared to the time of the New Testament when normally very little difference was made between illness and spirit possession. The doctor Johann Weyer (1515–1588) spoke out in his book "De Praestigiis Daemonum" against clerics who drove out demons if they meddled in medical affairs (De Waardt, 2005).

2.3.3 The Time of Enlightenment

It was often thought, before the Enlightenment, that it was evil spirits that made people ill and demon possession was given as a reason for mental illnesses. By the end of the 1700's however, this had almost ceased since significantly fewer people believed in demons and thus in demon possession (O'Grady, 1989). The Enlightenment increasingly encouraged human thought and reasoning, which in turn reduced the belief in the devil, demons and so on. Philosophers of the time derided the church's understanding of possession and thus the amount of public exorcisms greatly decreased. In areas however where Enlightenment thinking held little sway, or where it was deliberately resisted, there were spectacular cases of exorcism, even into the 18th and 19th centuries. The more liberal the theology became, the less seriously Satan and demons were counted on. In pietistic circles in southern Germany the ideas of the Enlightenment were resisted and against this background the famous battle between the Möttlinger vicar Johann

Christoph Blumhardt (1805–1880) and the demons of Gottliebin Dittus (1815–1872) took place. In this case she was finally freed of them after a struggle that lasted for months (Blumhardt, 1978). It was above all the emerging free churches (Mennonites, Methodists and Baptists) who held on tightly to their traditional biblical understanding and who continued to believe in the existence of the powers of darkness.

2.3.4 From the 19th Century Up to the 20th Century

It was Sigmund Freud himself who in 1923 in his paper "Eine Teufelsneurose im 17. Jahrhundert" (A Seventeenth-Century Demonological Neurosis) explained the possession of the painter Christoph Haitzmann as being a neurosis with suppressed instinctual impulses in the form of demonic expressions. Freud postulated that "the demons are evil, discarded wishes, progenies of rejected, suppressed instinctual impulses. We reject merely the projection into the outer world which the Middle Ages undertook with these spiritual beings; we leave them in the inner life of the invalids, where they dwell and come into being" (Freud, 1955). Many Protestant church circles adopted Freud's ideas whereas the free churches and Roman Catholic Church held on tightly to the concepts of Satan and spirit possession in the light of traditional biblical understanding, albeit in a modified manner. The Pentecostal movement which began to spread after 1900, developed the so-called deliverance ministry which the Charismatic movement brought even more into the spotlight from the 1960's and 70's onwards.

2.3.5 Deliverance Ministry in the 21st Century

In evangelical Christianity, convictions that were taken from the Bible were tightly held onto and so exorcism continued to be practiced, even if in different ways denominationally and exegetically; one now spoke of deliverance ministry, as mentioned above, in order to be isolated from the Catholic practice of exorcism. In particular the Pentecostal movement which had been expanding since 1900, and also the charismatic movement which had appeared since the 1960's, took the area of deliverance ministry under their wing. The Pentecostal movement has greatly aided the deliverance ministry of today. In Pentecostal churches, the supernatural aspect of Christian godliness was and is deliberately emphasised and encouraged. God's miracles are expected, supernatural gifts of the Spirit are practiced and the deliverance of demonised people is seen as a commission from Jesus. One cites Jesus' deliverance ministry and his promise in Mark 16:17, the deliverance ministries of Christians which were passed on to them in Acts and the statements of the apostle Paul in Ephesians 6 about the spiritual battle. The Pentecostal Church has not drawn up a standard teaching concerning deliverance ministry. When the charismatic movement began in the 1960's and 70's, the Pentecostal element was absorbed into the national and free churches and it was the latter who published more and more books about the ministry of deliverance. The literature dealing with deliverance ministry from the ranks of the charismatics describes various approaches, which are predominantly based on experience theology. There are moderate approaches to be found as well as extreme positions.

2.4 How do pastors diagnose spirit possession?

The answer to this question is closely linked to the denominational background of the pastor. A Roman Catholic priest, because of his theological orientation and the Catholic approach to exorcism[7] will proceed in a different way to a Protestant vicar who for example would sooner deny the existence of demonic powers, angels and Satan etc. and shift the topic into the area of psychology due to his or her historical-critical interpretation of the Bible.

Pastors within the free churches, especially from the Pentecostal-charismatic sphere, are as a rule considerably more active here since they acknowledge the reality of demonic powers and openly face this in their so-called deliverance ministry. They believe that God shows them (for example through prayer or the discerning of spirits) when it is a case of a spirit possession.

This thesis deals explicitly with pastors from free churches, and the interviews with free church pastors which will be examined more closely later in this thesis will show where the problems lie for these pastors. Before this is looked into, the dilemma they face will now be considered.

---

7 This will be detailed more extensively in the section "Theological Theories of Spirit Possession in the Roman Catholic Church in Germany".

2.4.1 The Dilemma of free church pastors

From a university background, Psychology and Theology are two completely different study courses. Both have a high intellectual and academic level. In Germany, Psychology is classified as a natural science and Theology as a humane discipline and officially the subjects hardly overlap. However, in pastoral every-day life, overlaps do occur again and again, particularly when people show symptoms associated with demonic possession. Both psychologists and ministers work predominantly with people: the former in clinics and practices and the latter in churches and schools (religion lessons). It can often happen that in the area of pastoral counselling, pastors are confronted with needs which perhaps psychologists could deal with better. Church members often go and see their minister first, and depending on their problems he can either help or he refers them to a psychologist. For if he suspects demonic possession then he will see himself more as a helper and less as a psychologist. Thus in the past, according to countless reports from ministers, it can be seen that it was not at all clear what actually the exact problem was. Famous cases such as that of Anneliese Michel show vividly how highly complex the situation can be. Here major exorcism was carried out several times by Catholic priests, but ultimately the woman died from malnutrition, and beforehand doctors had suspected epilepsy and mental illness. It is precisely in such particular situations, where psychology meets theology that theologians are in great conflict due to their lack of psychological knowledge. They are confronted with pastoral secrecy and the understanding of their faith on the one hand and the apparently obvious psychopathological recognisable needs on the other. With the exception of Catholic priests who have the "Rituale Romanum", there are no clear regulations or references as to how to work with people who report about demons etc. or who are regarded as demon possessed. Psychological guidelines for the diagnosis of mental disorders, such as ICD-10 and DSM-V, are unknown in the area of theology and thus better information would also help ministers here.

A result of my research work should therefore be that free church pastors receive assistance in this matter. Free churches across the world have no standard theological concepts, neither in their dogmatic, nor in their pastoral-theological disciplines.[8] No official guidelines such as the "Rituale Romanum" of the Roman Catholic Church[9] are available to them and thus the way they deal with the topic of spirit possession is also very diverse. The qualitative interviews with pastors from various free churches have confirmed this point.[10] In actual fact, this is exactly where the dilemma is found: On the one hand, one assumes from the exegesis understanding of the Bible that Satan, demons and spirit possession still exist, but on the other hand, one is not sure how to deal with this since no clear teaching on it has been given. In other words, the uncertainty is great in this area and this is also shown in the results of the interviews which will be expounded upon in the course of this thesis.

2.5 Religious and cultural expression of spirit possession

The relevance which respective cultures have in relation to spirit possession was pointed out in chapter 1.4 of this research. The way cultures deal with this topic varies according to how much a country or a region of the world has developed. In the second and third world countries it is nothing special to believe in spirits, gods and the supernatural, whereas in the western industrialised nations completely different statistics have been calculated (Belz, 2009). The situation is similar when it comes to religious perceptions in this context. In short it can be said that the religious intensity of people is directly connected to their religious-cultural life situation and that in religious areas of the world it is more likely that the topic of spirit possession is relevant than in areas where people are less religious. The respective religious contexts should be taken into account as much as the cultural contexts. Considering how greatly even world views vary from continent to continent, then it becomes clear how essential it is to understand the topic of spirit possession contextually. For this reason, the author undertook a two week trip to Africa in June 2015 in order to research into how spirit possession is dealt with in a different country with different cultural and religious beliefs.[11]

8 This will be detailed more extensively in the section "Theological Theories of Spirit Possession in Free Churches in Germany".

9 This will be detailed more extensively in the section "Theological Theories of Spirit Possession in the Roman Catholic Church in Germany".

10 This will be detailed more extensively in the section "Methodology".

11 The results of this research trip will be detailed later in this thesis.

2.6 Spirit possession in a theological-biblical perspective

2.6.1 Exorcism in the Old Testament

The existence of the devil is also mentioned several times in the Old Testament. His origin, his pride and his fall are described in Isaiah 14 and Ezekiel 28.[12] Exorcism in the sense of the driving out of a devil or demons does not however appear explicitly in any verses of the Old Testament. In the lexicon of theological terms, a number of examples concerning the belief in demons are listed: here it appears as a listing of demonic terms. In the Old Testament indications can be found of the general folk belief, for example in 1 Samuel 28:13 and in Isaiah 8:19. Demonic figures are referred to, such as schedim, s'irin, lilit, azälal in Isaiah13:32; 34:14. According to Deuteronomy 18:11; Leviticus 19:31 and 1 Samuel 28:3, invocation of the dead in Israel was forbidden, as well as sacrificing to evil spirits – Leviticus 17:7. Demons are spoken about in connection with Israel's worship of idols, and here the pagan gods are called contemptuous demons – Deuteronomy 32:17; 2 Chronicles 11:15; Psalm 106:37. Predominantly, however, is the tendency in the Old Testament to eliminate the belief in demons, such as in Genesis 1 where the heavenly bodies that are worshipped are described as lamps and are feared as demons in the Old Testament environment, or where the sinister and evil in 1 Samuel 16:14 and in 2 Samuel 24:1 – Satan, is attributed to God. The angels of Yahweh mediate between God and people, not demons. The Israelite is exhorted to turn to no other power other than Yahweh, and in particular he is to abstain from magic. In the LXX the term δαιμον (demon) appears only once, namely in Isaiah 65:11.

The strong retention of the Old Testament godliness was given up in Judaism and the belief in demons became more widespread, although the Jews never felt as greatly threatened by demons as the people of the surrounding religions. In addition, the scribes became involved in the belief in demons. The descriptions of demons are manifold: "schedim" = powerful ones, lords, demons; "mazziqin" = damagers; "mechabilim" = spoilers; "pega'im" = attackers; "s'irin" = male goat forms; "ruach ra'ah" = evil spirit; "ruach" = spirit. In previous times it was believed that according to

12 This interpretation of Lucifer is not shared by all theologians, but is accepted as real for this work.

Genesis 6:1 daemons came about as a result of the union between fallen angels and human women. One view of the origins of demons is that some of the people from the generation of the building of the tower of Babel were changed into demons; or that demons were produced from the intercourse of Adam and Eve with female or male spirits; or that demons are a special work of God's creation. Demons are spirits but have however physical organs (wings), need food and drink, can reproduce, are able to appear in human form and in other forms, too. Their number is infinitely large and they populate the world. The demon prince Aschmedai is at their head and under him is the smaller princess. Their dwelling places are on the earth as well as in the air, particularly in deserts, ruins and unclean places such as cemeteries. God gives them authority to carry out punishments which are imposed upon sinners. Although they belong to Satan's kingdom they can also kill. According to Genesis 4:26, their power began in the days of Enosh and will end in the days of the Messiah. Their main goal is to tempt people into sin. They cause many illnesses (but not all of them). God and the holy angels, God's word, keeping the commandments, amulets, and invocations etc. command and provide protection against demons.

In the people of Israel but also with Rabbis there is a great amount of sorcery and its application. In contrast to the Greek concepts, demons are not intermediate stages between God and man, nor are they spirits of the dead; angels and demons are sharply differentiated. It can be clearly seen that the Bible, as early as in the Old Testament, talks about Satan and mentions the existence of demons.

2.6.2 Exorcism in the New Testament

The New Testament takes the existence of demons for granted. Jesus often practiced exorcism in connection with the healing of certain illnesses. The evangelist Mark reports much about Jesus' exorcisms and even begins his report about Jesus' public ministry by writing about exorcisms: "So he travelled throughout Galilee, preaching in their synagogues and driving out demons."[13] It is further reported how Jesus drove out a demon, or rather demons (legion). Jesus' disciples also received authority to drive out demons

13 Mark 1:39.

(ecousia). In the missionary command in Mark's gospel, the sign of driving out demons is the first sign to be mentioned for those who believe: "And these signs will accompany those who believe: In my name they will drive out demons; they will speak in new tongues..."[14]

In Acts, the apostles Peter and Paul are familiar with the ministry of exorcism. Two terms appear in the New Testament in the case of when people are demonised: daimonizomai and echein daimonion. The term daimonizomai appears in the gospels of the New Testament 13 times. It means "to be possessed by a demon", "to be afflicted with a demon" or "to suffer from a demon". echein daimonion translated literally means "to have a demon". This term appears nine times in the gospels. Luke uses it parallel to daimonizomai (cf. Matthew 8:28 and Luke 8:27). Some exegetes assume there is a synonymous meaning of both terms and always translates the words with "possessed". Kraft (2000) alleges that, even if the intentions of the Biblical authors was possibly that daimonizomai was to show a somewhat stronger degree of demonic control than echein daimonion, this usage does not however justify translating one or the other of the two expressions as "to be possessed by demons". This translation contains the meaning "too much control". Based on this, the term daimonizomai is rendered by some Bible exegetes and translators as demonised, which contains the various degrees of demonisation – analogue to the various "being filled" with the Holy Spirit. Although the Holy Spirit is a godly person, the New Testament still describes that there is a filling with the Spirit. Paul encourages the Christians in Ephesus not to be full of wine, but rather to let them be filled over and over with the Holy Spirit.

In the science of religion, possession is described as an occupation of the person by a spirit. The question that arises from this for Christians is: Does the Bible also speak of a seizure and an occupation of a person by demons? There are no consistent answers to this question and often among evangelical Christians various perceptions become clear when this question is answered. It is without doubt that a person can be totally possessed by demonic powers, but as to whether this is always absolutely the case may not be assumed to be fact.[5] In the case of the two possessed men of Gardarenes

14 Mark 16:17.

in Matthew 8:28–34 it is obvious that these people were under the control of the devil. The example of the woman who had a "spirit of infirmity" cannot be classified so clearly. Just as difficult to classify are the other examples where Jesus speaks of a spirit of muteness, deafness or blindness. What about the woman in Acts 16 who had a spirit of fortune-telling in her and who followed Paul and Silas? In all these cases it "only" seems to be about a spirit of blindness, deafness, fortune-telling...possibly not then about a complete possession. The story of Ananias and Sapphira appears even more complex. These members of the first church in Jerusalem whose hearts were filled by Satan and who were not able to ask for forgiveness nor repent of their sins, but rather fell down dead. Is this a case of Christians who were possessed? For it says that their heart was "filled" by Satan. Or Simon the sorcerer who was converted after hearing Philipp's message, was baptised and is later described as someone who is "in bands and fetters of unrighteousness". In the letter to the Ephesians, Paul writes about a spiritual battle of faith for Christians. "For our struggle is not against flesh and blood, but against the rulers, against the authorities, against the powers of this dark world and against the spiritual forces of evil in the heavenly realms"[7]. He subsequently describes the spiritual armour which the believers should put on in order to be equipped for this battle. For Paul it seems that the spiritual battle of the individual believer against the powers of darkness was normal. Coenen (1993) phrases it in this way: "In the New Testament daimon (plur.) is only found in Mt. 8:31, otherwise daimonion is always used (63 times) or pneuma (spirit). No belief in the dead or in ghosts is to be found. Speculation about demons is absent. Angels and demons are antitheses. The fear of demons recedes as a result of the belief in the victory of Jesus Christ. Since communication with demons lies behind sorcery, the latter is rejected (Galatians 5:20; Revelation 9:20; 18:23; 21:8; 22:15). Pagan cult brings people into contact with demons (1 Corinthians 10:20), as indeed demons lie behind paganism (Revelation 9:20) and in the last days they will particularly become very active (1 Timothy 4:1; Revelation 16:13). Demons work in the present age (Ephesians 6:12) and give their wisdom (James 3:15), and this is why distinguishing between spirits is important (1 John 4:1; 1 Corinthians 12:10). The demonic powers are destined for judgment (Matthew 25:41; 8:29). 2 Peter 2:4 and Jude 6 speak of demons that have already been put in chains and are being kept for judgment.

Demons are subordinate to Satan, for they are his angels (Ephesians 2:2; Mark 3:20). They are not harmless. Above all they cause conditions of illness (Luke 13:11–16: the woman had a spirit of infirmity – Satan had bound her, cf. Acts 10:38; 2 Corinthians 12:7); but not all illnesses can be ascribed to demons. People who are possessed by demons appear in the gospels: people whose personality has been blanked out by evil spirits, and these speak through them (Mark 5:5). Because the sovereignty of God is in Jesus, he can break the power of the demons (Matthew 12:28) through his word of command (ekballo). The demons have superhuman knowledge: they recognise Jesus and know their fate (Matthew 8:29; James 2:19). Jesus himself is accused of having a demon (John 7:20; 8:48; 10:20). This is the hardest rejection of Jesus, being religiously justified, for in this case one wouldn't be allowed to listen to him. Against this accusation Jesus makes his calling clear that he honours the Father (John 8:49).

3 Psychological Theories of Spirit Possession

Chapter 3 describes the historic development of these psychological theories that are attributed for the phenomenon spirit possession. There exists a variation of attempts to explain this phenomenon out of the history from Freud and Jung to the current transpersonal psychology, conventional medical as well as recent attempts to explain as Weak Quantum Theory, the Model of Pragmatic Information and the parapsychological perspective.

Since the 19th century researchers have been trying to experimentally prove the existence of paranormal phenomena and as well as divination, bewitchment, psychic reading, there is spirit possession. Theories and models have been developed in order to draw our understanding as close as possible to these phenomena. What one has to bear in mind is that the scientific approach to investigations of human behaviour has drawn us closer towards evidence that is observable and tangible. In fact, Freud's theories created tension within the academic fraternity, for one cannot prove the unconscious in an empirical manner, and created a sense of dissonance between what can and cannot be investigated. Furthermore, the implication regarding the study of spirit possession is that it has come to be viewed in relation to that which is acceptable within academic traditions, meaning observability. In their book "Outside the Gates of Science", Borderick (2007), Radin (2006) and Jahn and Dunne (2006) provide a detailed overview about the theoretical approaches on this subject, going beyond the confines that scientific endeavour, as it is primarily and readily accepted, provides. The first section of the book is a recap of some of the most often cited evidence for ESP (Extrasensory Perception) starting with the work of Joseph Banks Rhine and his card-guessing experiments at Duke University. Broderick draws a firm line between this and previous research carried out by spiritualists and psychical researchers noting that the key distinction was one of method and perhaps more importantly, cast of mind. He argues that whereas nineteenth century psychical researchers resembled historians or geographical explorers accumulating anecdotes and taking copious notes to construct narratives, Rhine's 20th century laboratory-based approach emphasised scientific standards of rigour and repeatability.

Meanwhile three models have evolved which are currently being discussed and which Belz (2008) presents. These theoretical approaches enter a different path to that of traditional parapsychology. The latter assumed that paranormal phenomena, such as telepathy, precognition, psychokinesis or likewise phenomena of spirit possession, come about through transfer processes of information and energy. Attempts were made to explain these phenomena by using the so-called "signal transfer theory". Belz (2008) finds that these notions remain very widespread and that they also play a central role in esoteric and New Age concepts. However, and this point she emphasises, no signal of this sort could be found up to now in experimental parapsychological research. Modern experimental parapsychological research has to a large extent said its farewells to these concepts and has developed newer models which are derived from quantum mechanics. Research in the area of quantum physics has revealed completely new ways of dealing scientifically with things which cannot be or are extremely difficult to explain. Beltz finds that these models are clearly more fitting for the typical features of paranormal phenomena. At the Freiburg Institute (IGPP) and at the counselling centre run by Walter von Von Lucadou the findings of quantum mechanics are taken into account when it comes to explaining paranormal phenomena, or when advising people who report about such cases. For this, as much information as possible is obtained from the person seeking advice and then this is compared, or matched, with findings from quantum mechanics (in particular from general quantum theory).[15]

Belz explains how the behaviour of the phenomena can be characterised in the laboratory as well as in the field of research as follows: "They appear:

- suddenly and unexpectedly (spontaneously)
- without an obvious cause (acausality)
- to be independent of time and space (non-locality)
- to be fleeting and not easily replicated (elusivity)
- to have a particular meaning (evidence)
- to be made up of reasonable coincidences (coincidence/synchronicity)".[16]

15 This will be expounded more in Chapter 4.
16 Belz (2008). Extraordinary Experiences, p. 31.

This chapter will look at the spectrum of psychological theories and approaches concerning spirit possession. It will become clear that the schools of thought are spread over a wide spectrum as regards description as well as assessment and interpretations of spirit possession. Psychological theories have continued to develop throughout the course of history and it can be assumed that this process will also continue into the future. Different interventions will be arrived at according to the theory that is followed. A link should be made from the beginnings of mesmerism, from Freud and Jung across to the current theories concerning spirit possession. Before doing this, reference should be made to the thorough literature research of Dr. Pfeifer who in his paper "Demonic Attributions in Non-delusional Disorders" (Pfeifer, 1999) points out that there are effectively two main lines of theory about spirit possession. This was covered in detail in the previous chapters, but will be referred to again here for the sake of completeness.

The first line is the anthropological approach, which basically conveys that the respective culture is closely linked to the understanding and to the theory about spirit possession. The second line is more a medical-pathological approach which is more widespread in the western world. The four main theories (Culture-bound phenomenon, Witchcraft explanations, Hysteria and dissociation, and Delusion) were already presented in Chapter 1. Below follows the development to the widespread pure psychological theories, or the larger main lines of these, which are partly still represented today. The psychological approaches to spirit possession which are dying out due to increasing research development will also be presented. In this way a general overview will be ensured.

3.1 Hypnotism, hysteria and subconscious ideas

The roots of dynamic psychotherapy go back to the use of magnetism by Franz Anton Mesmer in the 1700's, where he proposed a new and different way of handling nervous disorders (Ellenberger, 1970), at the same time rejecting exorcism. In 1775, he made it his aim to show that he could produce the same curses in a person as the famous European exorcist, Johann Gassner. He believed that magnetic energy brought about nervous disorders that resembled spirit possession and he set out to physically alter this energy form. The disorders, he claimed, were caused by energy in the body, in fluid form, being unequally distributed. If equilibrium could be restored, by intervening and transporting the energy and depositing it elsewhere in the body, then the disorder could be cured. His attempts succeeded and led him to the belief that "demonic possession" could be scientifically and rationally explained and that an alternate medical treatment, not involving exorcism, could now be provided. His methods consisted of making magnetic passes with his hands over a patient's body, thus inducing magnetic sleep. Later these methods became known as mesmerism, but today this altered state of consciousness is now called a hypnotic trance. The characteristics of this trance are (Crabtree, 1985):

- Somnambulist state of sleepwalking
- Dual consciousness and memory
- Loss of identity
- Heightened long-term memory
- Sensory Blunting
- Extreme suggestibility
- Sensorial rapport
- Mental rapport
- Clairvoyance
- Transcendental awareness.

A basis for understanding spirit possession in a psychological way was thus laid by Mesmer through his discovery of trance states and his implications that humans have dual consciousness. Jean-Martin Charcot (1838–1893), a prominent hypnotist and neurologist, also played a role in explaining spirit possession scientifically (Ellenberger, 1970). His argument was that possession was merely a form of hysteria and "proved" this by generating and alleviating hysteria through the use of hypnosis. This idea was linked to psychopathology when he maintained that symptoms relate to the exclusion of ideas from personal consciousness: "The idea, like a virus, develops in a corner of the personality inaccessible to the subject, works subconsciously, and brings about all disorders of hysteria and mental disease" (Charcot cited in Ellenberger, 1970, p. 149). The devil was a manifestation of these solitary ideas, encountered as an isolated being due to its separation from the central ego. Pierre Janet (1859–1947), a French psychologist and psychotherapist, detailed the curing of a person who was spirit possessed using hypnotism and went on to give a more precise psychogenic explanation for possession. His interpretations were a precursor to the definitions that Freud was later to write about the unconscious:

"Man, all too proud, figures that he is the master of his movements, his words, his ideas and himself. It is perhaps of ourselves that we have the least command. There are crowds of things which operate within ourselves without our will" (Ellenberger, 1970, p. 370). Janet named these things "subconscious fixed ideas", proposing that they were caused by experiences that had been distressing or terrifying which then entered the subconscious and from this followed a psychological illness.

Multiple personality disorders and/or hysteria had, by and large, taken the place of spirit possession by the 1800's, although random cases of the latter were still recorded. An early discovery that came from hypnotism was dipsychism, i.e. that humans have a dual consciousness, the so-called "double ego". However, while carrying out hypnosis, the mesmerists observed that the person also displayed a third separate personality, as well as the waking and hypnotised personalities, which indicated that the mind was "rather like a matrix from which whole sets of subpersonalities could emerge and differentiate themselves" (Ellenberger, 1970). Consequently, dipsychism was replaced by polypsychism, the concept that the personality is a "multiplicity in a unity" (Ellenberger, 1970, p. 147), thus the ego is made up of numerous sub-egos with each ego having its own memory, awareness and consciousness. Spirit possession, seen as an ego-alien psychic manifestation, could now be understood in psychological terms.

3.2 The psychodynamic theories of Sigmund Freud and Carl Gustav Jung

3.2.1 Sigmund Freud

First of all, it has to be said that Sigmund Freud was very sceptical of religion, particularly of Christianity. For him religion was a "conceited rearguard battle" (Freud, S., GW 14, 431–432). Sigmund Freud developed the teaching of so-called demonical neurosis, about which he wrote, among other things, in the book "Eine Teufelsneurose im 17. Jh." (A Seventeenth Century Demonical Neurosis). Even in his introduction Freud makes it clear that one should not be surprised when the neuroses in earlier times appeared in a demonic guise. He criticises Charcot und his claims of linking spirit possession and ecstasy to hysteria and points out that it would have been easy to assign these cases of illness to a more precise diagnosis, namely that of neurosis. For Freud it is clear that "the states of possession correspond to our neuroses, for the explanation of which we once more have recourse to psychical powers. In our eyes, the demons are bad and reprehensible wishes, derivatives of instinctual impulses that have been repudiated and repressed. We merely eliminate the projection of these mental entities into the external world which the middle ages carried out; instead, we regard them as having arisen in the patient's internal life, where they have their abode" (Freud, 1923 p. 2). Even in his classics "The Interpretation of Dreams", "The Occult Meaning of Dreams" and "Dreams and Occultism" it is clear that essentially Freud was closely connected with the classical scientific world view. Telepathy in dreams or precognition was not imaginable for him and he didn't allow his renegade pupil Jung to persuade him otherwise. In 1932 he wrote in "Dreams and Occultism": "perhaps there is also within me the secret inclination to that which is wonderful, which accommodates the creation of occult facts". However, it becomes clear that he analysed everything critically. In one thing he finally gave in and in a letter from 1932 it can be read that he was prepared to believe that something new and important was concealed behind the so-called occult phenomena, namely the phenomenon of telepathy, i.e. the transfer of psychic processes to another person.[17] This side of Freud was actually hardly known about during his lifetime, as a protection against psychoanalysis being usurped by the sides of the occult sciences. The temptation to irrational belief in magic and the attempt to derive metaphysical theories had already played a part in his break with Jung who did not think as rationally about these matters as Freud. Academic circles had been deriding psychoanalysis for a long time by alleging it was close to occult practices, and in Austria a law had just been enacted that prohibited occult séances and the forming of spiritist sects. C.G. Jung, Freud's former pupil, went considerably further.

17 Quoted by C. Moreau, Freud et l'Occultisme, Paris: Privat 1976.

3.2.2 Carl Gustav Jung

C.G. Jung and his analytical psychology felt obliged to the "dark things" more than any other psychology movement. Whoever knows Jung's biography will not be able to avoid conjecturing how long and intensively this man concerned himself with the "shadowy sides of the human soul". In her biography of Jung "Memories – Dreams – Thoughts of C.G. Jung" (Rascher, Zürich, 1962), Aniela Jaffé, Jung's employee for many years, describes the analyst as a person who showed a life-long interest in occult and parapsychological matters. Even while he was studying, Jung read much spiritist literature and for many years visited mediums and sessions where contact was made with the dead. The fascination for everything supernatural was already evident with Jung's mother, Emilie Jung (1849–1923). She bequeathed a diary in which she reported exclusively about ghostly phenomena, premonitions and other "oddities" that she had experienced. Even Jung's grandmother, Augusta Preiswerk (1805–1862), was a "ghost seer".

After his separation from Freud in 1912, Jung developed his own approach which assumed that the psyche could transcend time and space. In 1920 Jung had a personal encounter with ghosts which he describes in more detail in the book "Spuk" by Fanny Moser (Moser F., p. 253–263). Together with colleagues (Schreck-Notzing und Eugen Bleuler), Jung carried out a series of experiments with the medium Rudi Schneider and was an eye-witness to materialisations, psychokinetic phenomena. In the 1930's, he repeated these experiments with another medium. In the preface to Stewart Edward White's book from 1948 "The Unobstructed Universe" Jung wrote: "I myself have not distinguished myself particularly in this area (of occultism) through original research, but I cannot wait so long to explain that I have observed enough of such phenomena to be fully convinced of their reality. They are inexplicable for me and so I cannot decide upon any of the usual explanations for them."

In particular in the last ten years of his work Jung worked together with Wolfgang Pauli, a physicist from Zürich who created the so-called "synchronicity theory as a principle of acausal connections". In 1952 this theory became widely circulated through the book "The Interpretation of Nature and the Psyche". Detailed definitions are also found in Jung's papers about essential concepts which are tailor-made for this thesis and will be elaborated upon in more detail in the following sections. Information can especially be found on this in the C.G.-Institutes (Zurich/Switzerland and Stuttgart/Germany), well-known in Europe, and in their libraries.

3.2.2.1 Spirit Possession

For Jung, spirit possession means that the self is taken over or fully occupied (possessed) by a complex or by another archetypical content. Possession for him is always slavery, bondage, subjection. Through it a person is restricted in the freedom of his will and decision. Similar to Freud, Jung claims that, for example in the case of hysteria, the human brain is "possessed" by this disorder. He also advocated Freud's theory that the characteristics of a neurosis in a modern person are essentially none other than the medieval form of spirit possession. However, he did not think much about the method of dream interpretation being used to examine the roots of this possession, something which Freud did. In the case of spirit possession, Jung orientated himself towards his so-called theological points of view, which implies that he had more an eye on the goals and intentions than on the causes of human suffering. From a personal discussion with Freud, it appears that Jung once brought up the question as to whether it did not lead to personal implications and possibly could make sense to fall prey to a neurotic possession.

3.2.2.2 The Shadow

In 1945 C.G. Jung wrote in detail about his understanding of the shadow. The shadow is that which a person does not want to be and thus summarises what Freud had already taught. The shadow is the negative side of the personality, the sum of all unpleasant characteristics which one would like to conceal, the worthless and primitive side of human nature, one's own second and negative self-personality, one's own dark side: the evil in a person. Here the Freudian school of thought shows through clearly. Jung himself said that the Freudian method represents the most detailed and deepest analysis of the shadow that is possible to attain. He still however deemed Freud's teaching about the shadow as limited and argued for a different approach. For him it was important to integrate the human shadow, to accept it. "The goal of analytical psychology in this area was thus to attain a confrontation with the shadow as part of the analysis with the acceptance of the shadow as the aim" (Samuels, Shorter & Plaut, 1989, p. 192).

3.2.2.3 The Evil

Concerning the concept of evil, Jung was convinced that there were far too many philosophical thoughts about it and that he himself would like to pursue a more empirical way. People's subjective judgment as to how they experienced good and evil was quite enough for him. Good and evil were principles of ethical judgments for Jung. He was often criticised by theologians since although he held on to the reality of evil, his conception of God was paradoxical in nature. Light and shadow, God and Satan, good and evil were a paradoxical unity for him. Jung discussed these topics in correspondence with a friend of his over a long period of time, the English priest Victor White, but finally they were not to see eye to eye concerning their views on the matter.

3.2.3 Transpersonal Psychology

Transpersonal psychology and transpersonal psychotherapy which builds upon this, try to expand classical psychology and psychotherapy approaches, according to their self-conception, with philosophical, religious and spiritual aspects. It developed from other psychological schools (psychoanalysis, behaviourism and humanistic psychology). Transpersonal psychology tries to describe spiritual experiences, including spirit possession, and to integrate them into existing modern psychology. There are many types of experiences that are observed and these include among other things mysticism, epiphany, altered states of consciousness, possession and trance. John Miller writes for the American Psychiatric Association (APA) that western psychology has the tendency to ignore the spiritual dimension of the human psyche (Miller, 1998). This is where transpersonal psychology begins. Transpersonal psychology however is not an independent concept, rather it is more a conglomerate of diverse psychological theories stretching from Jung (analytical psychology), across to Victor Frankl (logotherapy) and reaching Karlfried Graf Dürckheim (initiation therapy). Names like Abraham Maslow, Ken Wilber and, for about the last 20 years, Stanislav Grof also characterise transpersonal psychology. Much of that which transpersonal psychology conveys and teaches has been picked up and integrated by other psychological schools and therefore encounters increasing criticism from the advocates of pure science. Nevertheless, this theory will be presented here since it has a concept that concerns spirit possession.

Because of the central meaning of consciousness expanding experiences (through meditation, breathing techniques, such as holotropic breathing, but also through the taking of psychedelic substances such as LSD), encounters with good and evil deities, spirits etc. are not only accepted, but are also reported about by many representatives of transpersonal psychology, as well as taught and confirmed by clients. "Precisely spiritual people who through various methods find their way into these states of consciousness are the ones who have contact with powers of good and evil. Particularly with the so-called born again and death experiences. Most of the deities which one can experience directly in an exceptional state of consciousness, fall into two clearly separate groups: into the benevolent and benign deities, which are connected with the power of light and goodness, and into the terrible and ominous deities which represent the powers of darkness and evil" (Grof, 2013, p. 160–161).

3.3 Organic psychiatric interpretations

3.3.1 Dissociative Disorders

The area of dissociative disorders is described in ICD-10 under subparagraph F. 44. The states of trance and possession are also detailed here. The disorders in question are those where temporary loss of personal identity and complete awareness of surroundings occur. Literally this means: "in some cases the person behaves as if he is controlled by another personality, a spirit, a deity or a power". In the ICD it is explicitly written that only trance states can be included that "are involuntary and unwanted and which take place within daily activities, that is they occur outside of religious or other culturally accepted situations along these lines or at the most in connection with these" (ICD-10, 2005). Since these latter statements are directly connected to the phenomenon of spirit possession, as described up to this point, it becomes clear how difficult it is to set a boundary and how quickly a pastor can suspect spirit possession in a case of a dissociative disorder. This then supports the conclusion that pastors, due to their theological training in this specialised area, essentially lack psychological knowledge. This can lead to dramatic results in certain circumstances, as the internationally known case of Anneliese Michel has shown.[18] Conversely it can be inferred from this definition that every form of religious experience is classified outside of psychology, which in turn explains why it is that, especially in the western world, psychology has problems with the topic of spirit possession. Psychology will only focus on that which can be proven and the devil cannot be proven.

3.4 Weak Quantum Theory

Quantum mechanics is concerned with the subatomic particles in the universe. The generalised quantum theory is also called weak quantum theory because it handles weaker assumptions. The central concept here is *entanglement.* Entanglement means a non-local correlating of subsystems of a quantum system. It is said that particles which are in correlation with each other can no longer be viewed as being separate, even if they are spatially far apart. These entangled particles behave as if they are correlated, although neither signals nor energy are exchanged between them. This is called, as mentioned above, non-local correlation or entangled correlation. The generalised quantum theory describes complementarity and entanglement for all types of systems, for biological as well as psychological. Belz (2008) goes on to say that the complementarity principle, which was originally formulated by the physicist Niels Bohr (1927), is based on the interaction of incompatible or complementary properties of one and the same physical object (such as wave and particle properties), which are principally dependent upon each other by alternating. Heisenberg (1927) expresses these facts mathematically in the uncertainty principle where he postulates that the more precisely the position of a particle is determined, the less precisely its momentum is known, and vice-versa. The uncertainty principle is defined additively and its sizes are complementary and it is therefore possible for an entanglement. For Heisenberg it was clear that a very general complementarity prevails between material and spirit. The concept of entanglement had an influence on the Austrian Nobel Prize winner for physics, Schrödinger. With this he described the fact that two particles when they have once entered

18 Anneliese Michel was a German woman who underwent Catholic exorcism rites in 1975 and died the next year, due to lack of medical care.

into correlation with each other become components of an inseparable system and can no longer be observed as separate objects, even if they are spatially far apart from each other. "The generalised quantum theory predicts such entanglements in a narrower sense even in a generalised case in other quantum mechanics systems. Transferred into the environment, the coordination of psychic and biological processes as a type of generalised case of entanglement would be treatable."[19] This can be illustrated with an example. "A young man is seriously injured in a road accident in Australia. At the same time his sister who lives in Germany suddenly experiences, as if out of nowhere, intense feelings of fear accompanied by a feeling of sudden certainty that something has happened to her brother at this moment. This experience took place without there being any prior indication of this incident at that moment. Although at first independent of each other, both incidents (the serious road accident and the feelings of fear) are, for those affected by them, connected to each other as if over a bridge of the senses. In the context of generalised quantum theory, they are regarded as a non-local correlation in an entangled system. Such rational coincidences are preferential when reporting on crisis and danger situations, but also in the context of other mental instabilities, as they appear in altered states of consciousness, for example in meditative practices." Usually the advocates of this approach do not speak about deities, spirits or spirit possession, but since they try to explain things scientifically which are normally explained as supernatural or extraordinary, this scientific approach should be at least cited here, for it is an example of how the supernatural is explained naturally and thus loses its supernatural character.

3.5 Model of Pragmatic Information

The difference between the model of generalised quantum theory and the model of pragmatic information is that the psychological facts in the generalised quantum theory come off badly according to Walter von Lucadou (1997). He assumes that the reason why non-local correlations occur between complementary units in our everyday world is to be found in the fact that it is a matter of closed systems and also because further information

---

19 ibid. p. 34–35.

must exist which is meaningful for this system. This he describes as *pragmatic information.*[20] The condition of entanglement arises from this pragmatic information. For paranormal phenomena as well as for spirit possession this means that two mental and/or material elements can be correlated without spatial proximity or mediating elements being necessary (as for example with precognition). The theory of energy or signal transfer is therefore not needed here. The system remains a closed unity as long as the meaningful pragmatic information is kept constant, i.e. as long as no information is added or taken away. If paranormal phenomena actually correspond to non-local correlations, then it would be expected that when observing these they would disappear analogous to the measurement of an entangled physical system. Von Lucadou uses this as an argumentation in the following way: if for example researchers in a laboratory, but also therapists working with people with paranormal phenomena, are aiming to make these phenomena disappear (decline effect), they attempt to replicate the results or they challenge their patients to a precise observation of the extraordinary phenomena, i.e. looking for confirmation without novelty. The same applies when healers or mediums who claim to have particular paranormal abilities try to train these reliably and on an ongoing basis and to apply them as a method. This model can also explain a part of the influence experiences frequently reported by those seeking advice, which for example are reported after the termination of contacts with healers or after separations. Despite the formal termination of the relationship, perceptions in the model of self-continue to occur which are experienced simultaneously as external and as not belonging to the own self and are attributed to the former healer or partner. This entanglement can be solved according to the model of pragmatic information if the counselling process succeeds in generating meaning in the system, for example through a clarification orientated approach. With so-called precognitive dreams and premonitions, people normally only understand afterwards that what they thought or dreamt earlier could have a special meaning for them. According to the model of pragmatic information, extrasensory perception, for example, is not a classical transfer of information, but rather only a

20 von Weizsäcker, E. Novelty and Confirmation as Components of Pragmatic Information, p. 83–113.

non-local correlation, that is a simultaneous occurrence of meaningful events without a transfer of information being involved. Pragmatic information is subsequently the result, the product of something that happens for the very first time (novelty) and confirmation. Pragmatic information is particularly high when something is very new and at the same time maximally corresponds to the structures of the receiver. "This concept of information takes into account the actual content of meaning of a piece of information instead of only the quantity of signal units... The repeated reading of yesterday's newspaper reduces the novelty aspect by unchanging confirmation so that the pragmatic information increasingly sinks. If one, on the other hand, without knowing the Chinese language, reads a Chinese newspaper for the first time, the novelty is tremendously high, but the confirmation is zero. The highest measure of pragmatic information thus lies somewhere between absolute novelty and absolute confirmation."[21] Von Lucadou is therefore also one of the advocates who brings the supernatural onto a natural level. This is classically expressed in the title of one of his books: Geister sind auch nur Menschen ('Spirits are only people too').

Von Lucadou attempted for over decades to combine parapsychology with quantum physics and describes the weak quantum theory as "one of the most important theoretical works of parapsychology" (von Lucadou, 2012, p. 49).

3.6 Parapsychological theory

On 1st August 1921, Sigmund Freud wrote to Hereward Carrington: "If I had to live my life again, I would rather dedicate myself to parapsychology than to psychoanalysis".[22] "Parapsychology, the science of occult phenomena, is a young sub-discipline of the spiritual science, which deals with the research of controversial forms of experience and behaviour, both obviously exceeding the normal ability of awareness and the normal efficacy of the psyche and the body", this is how Hans Bender writes in his preamble to the book "Parapsychology – Development, Results, Problems".

21 Belz (2008) Extraordinary Experiences p. 36–37.

22 Quoted from Jones, who recognised the photocopy of this letter at N. Fodor cf. E. Jones, Volume III, p. 456.

3.6.1 History of Parapsychology

Phenomena which are nowadays called "paranormal" are reported of throughout the entire history of culture. The historical roots of parapsychology are to be found mainly in mesmerism and spiritualism. In 1862, the first "Ghost Club" was set up in England, consisting of a group of people who wanted to analyse apparitions. A systematic research in the parapsychological field began 20 years later. In 1882 the "Society for Psychical Research" (SPR) was founded in London and is still active today. The SPR was the first try to bring together scientists and scholars in one organisation, in order to ensure a critical and sustainable research of paranormal phenomena. Among the very first members of the SPR were philosophers, scholars, scientists, pedagogues and politicians like Henry Sidgwick, Arthur Balfour, William Crookes, Rufus Osgood Mason und Charles Richet. The first academical integration of parapsychology dates from 1927, this being the foundation of the parapsychological laboratory at the Duke University (Durham, North Carolina, USA) by the psychologist William McDougall (1871–1938) and the biologist Joseph B. Rhine (1895–1980). In 1911, the University of Stanford formed the first academical institution in the United States to research into extrasensory perception and psychokinesis in the laboratory. In 1930, the Duke University in Durham became the second biggest academic institution to strive towards research in extrasensory perception and psychokinesis in the laboratory. Under the guidance of the psychologist William McDougall and with the help of others, including the psychologists Karl Zener, Joseph B. Rhine und Louisa E. Rhine, the laboratory research into extrasensory perception began. Voluntary students were used as test subjects. Contrary to the approach of SPR and ASPR, who tried to verify the existence of paranormal phenomena based on qualitative evidence, the Duke University drew upon quantitative methods.

Parapsychological research spread all over Europe and in Germany "Institut für Grenzgebiete der Psychologie und Psychohygiene e.V." (The Institute for Frontier Areas of Psychology and Mental Health) was set up in Freiburg in 1950 and the "Abteilung für Psychologie und Grenzgebiete der Psychologie am Psychologischen Institut der Universität Freiburg" (Department of Psychology and Frontier Areas of Psychology at the Psychological Institute of the Universityof Freiburg) was founded in 1954, but was closed down in 2001. The "Parapsychologische Beratungsstelle" (Parapsychological Counselling Centre) of the Wissenschaftliche Gesellschaft zur Förderung der Parapsychologie (Scientific Society for the Advancement of Parapsychology) was also formed in Freiburg in 1989. Throughout Europe, the Freiburg group is seen as a leader in the field regarding the subject of paranormal experiences.

3.6.2 Current Status of Research

Parapsychological research is based on the one hand on the collection of so-called spontaneous reports, reports of extraordinary experiences, and on the other hand on the carrying out of experiments, where test subjects are examined with standardised tests. Recently the previous experiments of parapsychology have had to undergo a so-called meta-analysis, which clarifies the question if experimental results are "robust effects" or if they possibly just constitute experimental artefacts, which have resulted from methodical mistakes and/or selection. Various characteristics can nowadays be seen as verified.

Parapsychology obtains its material basically from three sources:[23]

- Spontaneous reports, i.e. descriptions of extraordinary experiences and activities, e.g. premonitions, real dreams, the "second sight", apparitions, ghostly phenomena
- "Qualitative" experiments with "sensitives" or "mediums"
- "Quantitative-statistical" experiments where non-selected test subjects are examined with standardised tests under strictly controlled conditions.

These tests stipulate the following variations:[24]

- "Telepathy": a test person (TP) (percipient/addressee) who is sensory well shielded tries to guess a sequence of well-randomised symbols which are viewed by a second TP (agent/sender)
- "Clairvoyance": the TP tries to guess the sequence of symbols "directly"
- "Precognition": the TP has the sequence of guessed symbols recorded before a relevant sequence is produced.

---

23 http://www.parapsychologische-beratungsstelle.de/Stand_der_Forschung/translated.
24 http://www.parapsychologische-beratungsstelle.de/Stand_der_Forschung/translated.

Initially the results were highly significant in the early days of the Rhine laboratory, however the following emerged: The more rigid the control conditions became, the more the hit performances approached the coincidence expectations, without the remaining "statistical anomalies" being able to be satisfyingly reduced to mistakes in planning, performance or evaluation of the experiment. Since the beginning of the 1960's, the "free-response" methods have gained relevance. These are basically a matter of three techniques:[25]

- The paranormal "manipulation" of dream contents under laboratory conditions
- Wholefield-Experiments: the eyes of the receiver acting as TP are covered by table tennis balls which are cut in half and illuminated by a light source. At the same time, the TP can hear random noise (wholefield situation, sensory deprivation) from a headset. This should create a "sensitivity" for psi-mediated impressions which are sent out from a transmitter by means of a predetermined target image
- "Remote-Viewing": Experiments where the "receiver" tries to reproduce the awareness of a "sender" who is located at a randomly selected place.

The question of psychokinesis was evaluated by J.B. Rhine using the cube experiments which he invented himself. Since 1970, more and more electronical and quantum-physical random generators have been in use: The TP receives the instruction to direct a sequence of events, e.g. the illumination of little ring like arranged lamps that have been created by the random generator, in a given direction, e.g. clockwise direction, just by the efforts of his will.

3.6.3 Criticism of parapsychological theory

Over the course of time, parapsychology led a shadowy existence in the light of the "genuine, scientific" psychology. Even though diverse institutes were founded in order to try to establish parapsychology as an independent scientific branch of psychology, more and more critical voices spoke up and also various university chairs disappeared, since they could not be retained financially. The zenith of parapsychology in the European countries seems to be over.

25 http://www.parapsychologische-beratungsstelle.de/Stand_der_Forschung/translated.

Most important in this regard is the foundation and development of the Society for the Scientific Investigation of Parasciences (GWUP).[26]

The well-known American psychologist and sceptic Ray Hyman imparted his assessment of parapsychology in the British magazine Sceptic (2/2010) under the headline "The Demise of Parapsychology" (Hyman, R. (2010): The Demise of Parapsychology, 1850 – 2009. Sceptic 22(2) 17–20.) Hyman has critically accompanied parapsychology for decades and due to the fact that he was also a valued partner in discussions for parapsychologists, experts were astonished that he came to the conclusion that it was time to testify to the death of this "160 year old undertaking" (Sceptic 2/2010). Hyman summarised what other scientists also say, namely that parapsychology stepped up in the 19th century in order to provide scientific proof of the existence of spiritual, that is occult, phenomena. This should have convinced the scientific community, who was already sceptical at that time, of the existence of psi and the paranormal. Over the past ten years, more and more parapsychologists have come to see that this target is not reachable (e.g. Bierman 2001; Jahn, Dunne 2008; Kennedy 2001, 2003; von Lucadou 2001), according to Hyman. These neo-parapsychologists, as Hyman calls them, need to admit that the situation of proof for psi and the paranormal is not only contradictory and elusive, but also does not comply with scientific standards.

While this was formerly regarded as a drawback, parapsychologists now claim that psi can generally not comply with scientific standards: they argue that it lies in the nature of psi that it is not even within the reach of scientific methodology. The original ideal of parapsychology would have been lost with the demand derived from this, i.e. that the scientific method must be given up, that is, must be adapted to the requirements of parapsychology. Certainly there would still be parapsychologists (like Jessica Utts or Dean

26 GWUP is a member of the European Council of Sceptical Organisations (ECSO), which also contains a list of member organisations in Europe. The ECSO site also shows a list of ongoing and planned events in Europe and worldwide. You can find more information on issues related to sceptics organisations in English at the websites of the Committee for Sceptical Inquiry, the Sceptics Society and the James Randi Educational Foundation. For a complete list of sceptics' organisations around the world, please consult the list maintained by the UK sceptics organisation ASKE, also a member of ECSO.

Radin) following the original scientific paradigm, who believes that the existence of psi was scientifically proven. But Hyman contradicts this argument. Too often parapsychologists rely only on meta-analyses and these suffer from notorious problems (Sceptic 1/2005). To some extent the used studies would be cleverly combined so that, in the end, it looked as if there was nevertheless proof of an effect. Furthermore, the Decline-Effect – the decline of the intensity of effects in relation to increasing and improved research – would be a sign of the non-existence of the assumed subject of parapsychology. If you were to really come up against a robust, replicable effect, the intensity of effects would normally have to show an increase. Finally, you would have to state that the subject of parapsychology – the ominous psi – is still defined in an absolutely negative way (Alcock 2003). The absence of a positive characteristic would lead to the fact that you simply cannot tell if an effect discovered in one experiment is really based on the same cause as an effect in another experiment.

Based on this and many other reasons, said Hyman, parapsychology, in his opinion, could not meet its claim to prove the paranormal with scientific means. If the neo-parapsychologists now interpret the eccentric behaviour of parapsychologic results as an indicator that the unreplicability, irregularity and volatility are part of psi's nature, they admit the failure of parapsychology, said Hyman. With their demand to alter, that is to weaken, the scientific methods (see particularly Jahn, Dunne 2008) in order to help psi to gain recognition, they turn away from science and return to occultism. In this case, said Hyman, you can only come to the conclusion that parapsychology after 160 years has bitten the dust. The psychologist Wiseman agrees with Hyman to a large extent, but is prepared to give parapsychology a very last chance and challenges it to determine the experiments with the most promising approaches and to try to replicate them in one concerted action in several laboratories simultaneously under very strict conditions. If this doesn't lead to success, you should finally accept the null hypothesis – psi doesn't exist. Parapsychologists like Watt and Roe, as well as the scientists at IGPP in Freiburg, don't agree with Hyman's analysis and they see an ongoing demand for further research.

To summarise it can be said that (over decades) there have been and there still are many efforts to explain the phenomenon of spirit possession scientifically. Everything can be found, from psychological, to quantum physical and to parapsychological approaches – and each particular representative essentially has a good explanation. But are these explanations really adequate? In any case, it makes clear that spirit possession is a very complex subject.

What also has to be considered in this regard are the theological approaches, which will be detailed in the following chapter and which approach the subject from totally different basic positions.

Principally the question can be asked as to whether you can actually explain and understand something that possibly cannot be explained or needs no explanation at all. Here natural science meets the humanities, psychology meets theology. One can only guess how great the challenge is for pastors who come into contact with these phenomena.

4 Theological Theories of Spirit Possession[27]

This chapter discusses some of theological theories regarding spirit possession. Special reference is made to the current position of the Protestant and Catholic churches in Germany as well as the charismatic movement. In addition, free church associations' position on spirit possession will be explored.

There is no simpler way to state what theology is than to describe it as the doctrine of God. The basis of theology on the one hand is the Bible[28] and on the other hand the theological writings of 2000 years of history of the church. As much as there is not only one theological doctrine, there is also not only one church. This has a direct influence on the theological doctrines about spirit possession.

The theological history of spirit possession has already been detailed in Chapter 2 of this thesis, therefore this chapter will deal with the current theological theories of spirit possession. These theories are closely associated with the particular denomination. Against this background, the current situation in Germany shall be described. This will help to understand the methodology (Chapter 5) and the analysis of the interviews with free church pastors in Germany.

4.1 Theological Theories of Spirit Possession in the Protestant Churches in Germany

In Germany, the landscape of churches is characterised in a very special manner. This has historical reasons and differs from other countries. In Germany, up to the time of Martin Luther, there was only the Holy Catholic Church (as the Catholic creed still says today and as it is spoken and prayed every Sunday in the Catholic mass).

Through Martin, the reformation took place in the 16th century and by degrees a second large church developed in Germany, the Protestant Church[29].

27 The author is deliberately concerned with Christian theology.

28 In Protestant churches and free churches, the biblical canon consists of Old and New Testament, altogether 66 books. In the Catholic Church, the Apocrypha are added.

29 This thesis uses the word "Protestant Church".

In Germany, there is the Catholic Church and the Protestant Church (each federal state has its own Protestant Church).

Every two years, the "Forschungsgruppe Weltanschauungen in Deutschland" (fowid)[30] (Research Group for World Views in Germany) publishes up-to-date figures on the religious status in Germany, see below a chart for 2014.

Figure 1: Religious proportional distribution in Germany 2014[31]

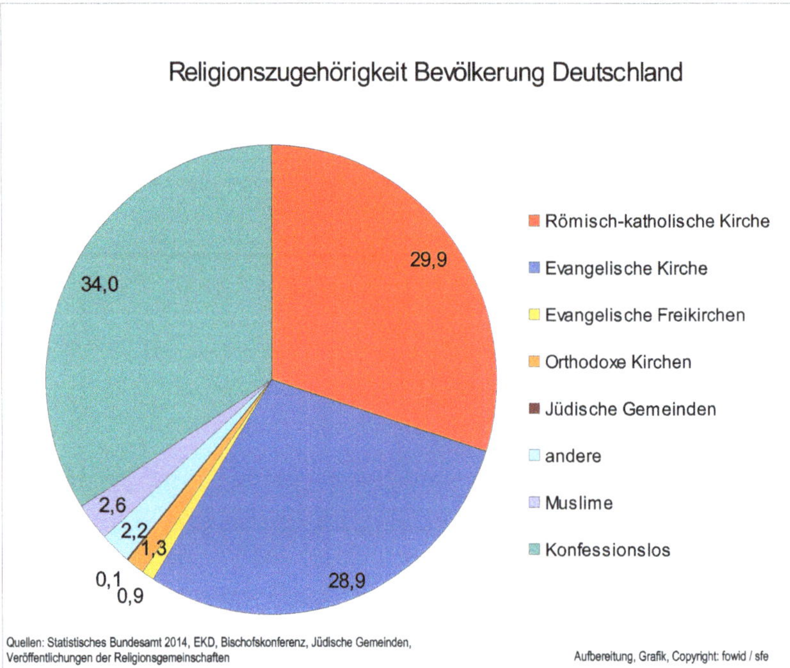

34.0 m	No Confession/Denomination	2.2 m	Others
29.9 m	Roman Catholic Church	0.9 m	Free Churches
28.9 m	Protestant Church	1.3 m	Orthodox Churches
2.6 m	Muslims	0.1 m	Jews

30 The "Forschungsgruppe Weltanschauungen in Deutschland" (fowid) (Research group for world views in Germany) pursues the goal of collecting data for comprehensive empirical information regarding all aspects of different philosophies – either of religious or political character – and to evaluate and summarise them in order to make them accessible to the public.

31 http://fowid.de/ 09/05/2015.

The Protestant Church in Germany and its theologians have delivered only a few statements on the subject of spirit possession over the last few decades. Certainly the Church knows about the Lutheran writings on Satan and his nature and actions, however they are considered to be located in the medieval world view and are therefore no longer taken seriously.

The Protestant theologians Althaus and Thielicke[32] saw demonic spirits acting in history during the time of National Socialism and Karl Barth talked about Satan as of the "void" and tried to interpret Satan's nature and origin, as well as the divine and the creatural, in that way. Current theologians essentially do not have a position on this subject, at least in the German region. This is possibly due to the fact that the Protestant Church never developed a binding ritual that would be even slightly comparable to the "Rituale Romanum"[33]. Althaus writes: "In particular, the biblical demonism indeed shows streaks of primitive mythology that are dismissed by us... As a result, we do not regard illnesses in an exorcistic way. On this point the world view of the Bible is something of the past for us. The true reason for the knowledge about Satan must be carefully separated from the rest of primitive thinking. On the other hand it does not count against the validity of the thoughts on Satan in the New Testament that it is interwoven with primitive-mythological traits. Also the appreciation of the power of Jesus to heal as a sign of the coming of the Kingdom of God is not bound to the demonological, that is exorcistic, interpretation of illness or healing as Jesus shared it. The same applies to Blumhardt"[34] (Althaus, 1948).

Another German theologian, Rudolf Bultmann[35], goes even further in his understanding as he writes: "Nevertheless, I claim that the prospect of demons in the New Testament is perfect superstition if it lives on or is revived in the modern world; the church should immediately do its best

32 Paul Althaus, 1888–1966, and Helmut Thielicke, 1908–1986, were important Protestant theologians.
33 Rituale Romanum will be explained in the next section.
34 Johann Christoph Blumhardt, 1805–1880, was a Protestant pastor who performed exorcisms on Gottliebin Dittus for months. These were well documented and confirmed by the official church.
35 Rudolf Bultmann, 1884–1976, Protestant theologian with his own concept of the "Demythologisation of the New Testament".

to exterminate it because it can only endanger the true effectiveness of the Kerygma. Blumhardt's stories are an aversion to me" (Bultmann, 1948).

Quite different is the position of the theologian Adolf Köberle who thinks that it is not impossible that there are "borderline cases of extreme darkness and weirdness, where you cannot get by with these immanent interpretations, where there is nothing else for it but the bitter and frightening thought that an external occupation has taken place here" (Köberle, 1974).

The commissioner for sects and philosophy of the Bavarian Protestant church, Pastor F.-W. Haack, said about the activities in Klingenberg concerning Anneliese Michel in 1976[36]: "I refuse exorcism with one single exception: I believe that, once applied, it can be a mental stopgap assistance in certain cases, but only in cooperation between pastor and psychotherapist" (Haack, 1976).

In 2013, an article by the theologians Haringke Fugmann and Harald Lamprecht was published with the title "Possession and Exorcism from the Protestant Point of View", which illustrates Protestant perspectives on the phenomenon of spirit possession. Theological and non-theological approaches are stated therein and at the end, pastoral recommendations are given. Jesus as an exorcist is discussed as well in Augustinus' conception of demons.

Also the exorcism of the Roman Catholic Church is explained and finally today's practice of deliverance ministry is introduced. The summary of Fugmann and Lamprecht reveals that the belief in spirit possession did not lose anything of its fascination and that both the Enlightenment and a high educational standard could not avoid this happening. Jesus' exorcism is historically recognised. What increasingly happened in the Middle Ages was that exorcism as a therapeutic measure became an instrument to distinguish the spirits (Fugmann & Lamprecht, p. 22). It is seen as a problematic consequence that all phenomena that are not explicitly divine are pinned on Satan. Charismatic and Catholic understanding of exorcism are seen as similar, for example when it is claimed by these circles that it can only be a case of possession when it has been "proved" that there are neither physical nor mental

36 Anneliese Michel was a German student who died in 1976 as a consequence of extreme malnutrition. This case attracted worldwide attention because in the months before her death, two Catholic priests performed all in all 67 times the large exorcism on her.

causes and illnesses, which encourages an unhealthy black and white thinking (Fugmann & Lamprecht, p. 23). The German theologian and pastor Hans-Jörg Bräumer commented: "The demons belong to the realm and the power of Satan. Their activity is extensive. They operate in the background of the world and of mankind. They have a powerful influence on the arrangement of public conditions. They feel a passionate urge to embody themselves in human beings and can cause awful tortures and symptoms of illnesses. The demons destroy the human likeness of God. The core personality – the ego of a human being – his conscious desire and action is paralysed by them. Demons finally chase the human being into self-destruction. The ego of a human being can be turned off to such an extent that the demon appears as the subject of speaking" (Bräumer, 1976). In this way Bräumer supports a point of view that Dr. Kurt Koch already postulated.

4.2.1 Dr. Kurt Koch

The Protestant pastor and theologian published many works about pastoral counselling and occultism, travelled to more than 100 countries and added the following sub-title to his 700 page book "Pastoral Counselling and Occultism: A study in consideration of internal medicine, psychiatry, psychology, depth psychology, religion psychology, parapsychology, theology".

To him, Satan and demons were an inviolable reality, in theory as well as in practice. Many Christians have read both of his standard works "The Occult ABC" and "Pastoral Counselling and Occultism" and have been influenced by them, but this however not in the whole Protestant area, but more in the evangelical circles[37] of Germany in the 1960's and 1980's. Criticism was predominantly directed at Koch from his theological colleagues within the Protestant Church, whereas in evangelical circles he was popular and valued. In order to make his theological position as well as his frequent interactions with psychologists and psychiatrists understandable, reference is made to the following autobiographic report by Koch:

37 The term 'evangelical' (not to be compared with Protestant) describes a Christianity independent from any confessional affiliation, that refers to the Bible as its sole statement of faith and that makes a distinction between mere ecclesiastical traditions on the one hand and from secularisation on the other hand.

It was more than 20 years ago. Professor Bender had invited me to talk about the problem of spirit possession in his institute in Freiburg[38]. Also invited were some psychologists, Catholic theologians and a professor form the psychiatric clinic. After the speech there was a discussion about a female patient from the psychiatric clinic who showed symptoms of an illness that were unknown to the psychiatrist. The patient would suddenly cry out and declare that she was being beaten by invisible powers. Traces of blows showed up on her body. On another occasion she seemed to be overwhelmed by a large snake. The windings of the snake were photographed by an assistant doctor. The psychiatrist explained these phenomena as psychogenic conditioned demographic (mentally conditioned changes of the skin). Once a nurse tried to protect the patient and put her arms around her. Then the nurse was beaten too. The psychiatrist explained this as a mental induction (transfer). Sometimes male voices talked out of the patient impersonating seven devils. The psychiatrist called this process dissociation (splitting up) of the unconscious into seven independent parts. Occasionally clairvoyance phenomena also occurred. The professor asked the Catholic theologians who were present for their opinion. They stated: 'This is spirit possession'. The psychiatrist was a little agitated and answered: "Your bishop already suggested this in his covering letter. I do not believe it is so. At the most this is for me a case of hysteria, certainly in a form that I have not known up until now." Then he also asked me for my opinion. First of all I asked a counter question: "Do you know if this woman dealt with magic or spiritism?" The answer was positive. Then I expressed my conviction that we were facing a case of spirit possession here. Later I learned that this woman had committed herself to Satan with her blood. It can be fully understood that scientists are afraid to acknowledge a case of spirit possession. Spirit possession is not a medical term but a religious one. What however is difficult to understand is that most of the theologians let themselves ride on psychiatrists' and psychologists' coat-tails; here it is not only modern theologians who are meant but also those who have a good name in the church of Jesus. The condemnation by the "guild" sciences is also the reason why theologians hardly dare to write a book on spirit possession. The most

38 This concerns the IGPP, already mentioned in Chapter 3.

important books to me are: Biblical Demonology by Dr. Merrill F. Unger; Demons in the World today by Dr. Merill F. Unger; Demon Possession by John L. Nevius. The discussion with psychiatry would require too much space. It would also be unsuccessful. A psychiatrist who is not a Christian or just a nominal Christian cannot be convinced of the existence of spirit possession. Some arguments shall be mentioned anyway.

1. Psychiatrists state that Jesus and his followers were children of their time. They did not know better. What they regarded as spirit possession was in fact a mental illness. I have heard this argument ad nauseam. And it is so easy to disprove it. Jesus, his followers and the writers of the New Testament's scriptures differentiated very well between illnesses and demonical possession. Illness and possession are clearly distinguished in the following Bible passages: Mt. 4:24; Mt. 8:16; Mt. 10:1; 10:8, Mk. 1:32; Luke. 9:1–2 and in other passages.

2. The reactions of mental patients and those possessed are different. I don't want to repeat at this point what I have published in other books. In the book entitled 'Demonology, Past, and Present', from page 136 onwards, I have quoted eight signs for possession. Here only a few main characteristics shall be mentioned:

a. The fits of raving madness that occur only under clerical supervision. I was called to a woman who started to riot if someone tried to pray with her. She did the same with me. In such cases I used commands in the name of Jesus.
b. The trance. If you want to pray with a person who has brought himself under a curse through spiritualism, they immediately fall into a trance. In Zurich, a preacher brought a woman to me for pastoral counselling. When I prayed with her, she fell into a trance and poked her tongue out at me. When I said 'Amen', she regained consciousness. I asked her if she had visited spiritualistic sessions. She confirmed this. For nine years she had belonged to a circle.
c. The speaking of languages that have not been learned. This is also regarded as a sign of possession in the Rituale Romanum.

Koch writes: One day, a young man came to me for pastoral counselling. During the prayer he fell into a trance and the voices that spoke out of him used foreign languages that the young man had not learned. This is the strongest argument against the psychiatrists' position. A mental patient does not suddenly speak foreign languages that he has not learned. The symptoms of mental illnesses and of possession are different. A gleam of light occurs on the horizon in a book entitled 'Emotion and Possession', published by Jürg Zutt (A.-Francke-Verlag, Bern/München 1972). The articles are the transcription of psychiatric and anthropologic speeches on the occasion of the conference of the World Psychiatric Association and the Werner-Reimers-Foundation for anthropologic research. At this congress, psychiatrists, psychologists, sociologists, theologians, medical historians and anthropologists had a chance to speak. A partial result of these symposia (conferences) was that the following was declared: For the time being you need to make yourself comfortable with the thought that emotion and possession need to be assessed independently in their religious aspect and may not be labelled in a quickly drawn conclusion as a mental illness.

This is an astonishing concession. However, this is something that believing Christians have known for a long time without having studied medicine, psychology or anthropology. After long detours, science gradually arrives at the point where the faithful have been holding the biblical position for two millennia (Koch, 1982).

Kurt Koch's positions are partly opined to the present day and in the course of this chapter they will be enlarged upon. On the whole it can be assumed that the current Protestant position is closer to that which is seen from the scientific background: Possession phenomena are severe mental illnesses and cannot be traced back to demons or similar things. Thus exorcism is not necessary (exorcism being neither taught nor practised in the Protestant Church, in contrast to the Catholic Church), but what is needed is medication or hospital treatment in appropriate clinics.

4.2.2 The Charismatic Movement within the Protestant Church

Within the Protestant Church in Germany there is a movement which calls itself "Spiritual Renewal of the Church" and is part of the worldwide charismatic movement. These believers are baptised members of the Protestant Church, and thus Protestants, but however are open in their theological orientation for the supernatural working of God, for worship, and they practise the gifts of the Spirit and believe in the works of the devil and demons and in the deliverance from these powers. They assume, in their theology, that people can be possessed. They orientate themselves using the teaching on deliverance ministry in a charismatic context. It is thus assumed that people, including Christians, can be under the influence of demonic powers and that these burdened or possessed people need deliverance. This deliverance ministry normally takes place using commanding prayer and the laying on of hands, often in conjunction with fasting. The statements in the New Testament are referred to and various needs, problems, psychic-social disorders as well as physical illnesses are attributed to demonic powers. An example of a current German representative of this is the "Joshua Ministry" whose founder is Dr. Christoph Häselbarth.[39] In his publications (as in many other charismatic books) he writes much about Satan and demons and how deliverance ministry can be precisely carried out. In his brochure "Called to Freedom" he lists names of demons in the appendix: death, suicide, murder, destruction, violence, darkness, deceit, lies, anger, rage, hate, retaliation, irreconcilability, bitterness, rebellion, obstinacy, rejection, fear of rejection, fear, terror, agony, gloom, isolation, self-rejection, worthlessness, guilt, shame, embarrassment, sensitivity, anxiety, confusion, frustration, adultery, temptation, rape, abuse, depression, defeat, nervousness, doubt, unbelief, scepticism, pride, arrogance, vanity, perfectionism, insecurity, competitiveness, illness, blasphemy, swearing, mockery, coercion, control, dominance, depiction, sexual fantasies, homosexuality, alcohol, drugs, nicotine, addictions, craving for food, anorexia, bulimia... He names the following as occult/cultic spirits: Free Masonry, Christian Science, Scientology, Jehovah's Witnesses, New Age, Rosicrucian Order, Unitarianism, Mormons, Buddhism, Islam, Hinduism, Shintoism, Ouija board, horoscopes, magic, astrology, fortune telling, palm reading... (Häselbarth, p. 54–56)

39 The Josua-Dienst e.V.(Joshua ministry) is a non-profit organisation with a free, non-denominational, Christian basis and is predominantly active in the areas of biblical Christian counselling, pastoral work and training. The organisation was founded in 1989 by Dr. Christoph und Dr. Utta Häselbarth.

As a classical representative of the charismatic movement,[40] Häselbarth points out practical steps as to how people can be delivered from demons.

In order to obtain an understanding for the theological teaching and practice of deliverance ministry, his concept of the deliverance from demons and that of Derek Prince[41] will be shown as an example for the charismatic movement. Even if the points are not always 100% identical, the principle will be clear. Häselbarth teaches 12 steps to deliverance:

1. Our position in Jesus
2. Humble oneself before God
3. Confess all sins
4. Repent from all sins
5. Forgive all other people involved
6. Isolate the powers and point out their limits
7. Loosening of false bonds and objects
8. Release from curse(s) on one's life
9. Take a stand together with God and resist the devil
10. "Casting out" of the enemy
11. Pray for inner healing
12. Thank Jesus and give him all the honour (Häselbarth, p. 40–47)

These 12 steps are intensively discussed with the people seeking advice and the relative results spoken ("your sins are forgiven", "you have forgiven everyone", "I cut through these bonds", "I absolve you from this curse" etc.).

Derek Prince recommends nine steps in his book "They will drive out demons":

1. Strengthen your personal faith in Christ
2. Humble yourself
3. Confess every known sin

---

40 Other representatives are: Derek Prince, Charles Kraft, John Wimber, Dennis Bennet, Wolfhard Margies, George Mallone, Lester Sumrall, Timothy Warner, C.P.Wagner, James Stanton, Peter Horobin, Ken and Silvia Thornberg and many more.

41 "Derek Prince (1915–2003) was educated at Britain's finest universities. While serving in the British army during World War II, he experienced a life-changing encounter with Jesus Christ. He then devoted his life to the teaching and study of the Bible and became internationally recognized as a leading authority on Bible prophecy. His daily radio program continues to touch lives around the world."

4. Repent from all sins
5. Forgive all other people
6. Break with the occult and all false religions
7. Pray for release from every curse upon your life
8. Take a stand together with God
9. Cast out (Prince, p. 244–256)

The charismatic movement's understanding and its view of spirit possession becomes clear through both these practical procedures. It is assumed that one of the central tasks of Christianity is to drive out demons and various statements are referred to in the New Testament to justify this.[42] These approaches are viewed very critically by the non-charismatic sections of the Protestant Church and the charismatics are accused of over-enthusiasm and one-sided interpretation of the Bible.

4.3 Theological Theories of Spirit Possession in the Catholic Churches in Germany

The Roman Catholic Church with its 1.2 billion members worldwide is the biggest Christian denomination in the world. It has the longest church history and considers itself to be a "mother church" and attributes the papacy directly to the apostle Peter. Concerning the topic of spirit possession, it has the longest tradition. In the first centuries after Christ each church already had its own exorcists and the latter are still present in the Catholic Church at the present time. In 2014, the Vatican officially recognized the "International Association of Exorcists". Dioceses in southern Europe and South America wanted to react to a strengthening in occultism and thus their requests were granted. The aim in recognising this association is that the exorcists are better controlled by the church and that sensationalism, such as with exorcisms that could have come straight out of a film, is prevented. At the same time exorcists admit that evil takes "possession" of a person in just one in a

42 "I have given you authority to trample on snakes and scorpions and to overcome all the power of the enemy" (Luke 10:19).
"And these signs will accompany those who believe: In my name they will drive out demons" (Mark.16:17).
"When he had called the Twelve together, he gave them power and authority to drive out all demons" (Luke 9:1).

thousand cases. Thus it is important to work closely together with psychoanalysts und psychiatrics. This is also the requirement of the founder of the association, Gabriele Amorth, who was born in Modena in 1925, and who was its president from 1994 until 2000. Also a graduate in law as well as a priest, Amorth was officially appointed as the exorcist of the diocese of Rome in 1986. Around 250 exorcists from 30 countries belong to the association. It now has the canonical status of a "private club of believers" and is its own entity; the club however does not have an official character and cannot act "in the name of the Church" (L'Osservatore July, 2014).

The year 1614 was an important year historically, since as a result of the Council of Trient various liturgies of the Catholic Church were reformed and in the course of this a decisive "new beginning" ensued for exorcism. The "Rituale Romanum" was introduced.

4.3.1 "Rituale Romanum"[43]

The "Rituale Romanum" was an attempt to curb the proliferation in exorcisms and to find a general binding clerical standard for the church. In contrast to the minor exorcism from Pope Leo XIII which every Catholic layman may practice (however only upon himself), the major exorcism can only be performed by a priest with appropriate training and special permission from a bishop. Precise procedures and prayer texts are given in order to free people out of the hand of the devil or demons. These regulations were valid for over 300 years and were also practised, until the "Rituale Romanum" was revised in 1952 and this version remains valid today. Essential prerequisites are three indications which serve to determine whether a person is actually possessed:

1. The person who is possessed speaks in a language that is foreign to him or understands such a language.
2. The person can disclose remote or hidden things.
3. The person shows supernatural physical strengths.

43 This has already been detailed in Chapter 2.3.3 and hence an essential summary appears here.

There follows an excerpt from Tit. XII, 2 of the "Rituale Romanum" in order to provide an insight into this form of exorcism:

"I adjure you, old serpent, by the judge of the living and the dead, by your creator, by the creator of the world, by Him who has the power to send you into hell, that you, filled with fear, with the whole legion of your terror, flee from this servant of God, who returns to the fold of the church. I adjure you once again (the exorcist makes the sign of a cross on the forehead of the possessed), not through my weakness, but through the power of the Holy Spirit that you get out of this servant of God, whom the almighty God has created in His image. Go away, not from me, but from this servant of Christ. The power of Him crushes you who has subjugated you by His cross. Tremble before the arm of Him who has conquered the raging of the underworld and has led the souls to the light. Terrible is the human body (sign of the cross on the breast), dreadful the image of God (sign of the cross on the forehead). Do not resist, do not hesitate to leave this person, for it has pleased Christ to live in a person. Do not believe that you could resist by deeming me to be far too great a sinner. God commands you. The majesty of Christ commands you. God the Father commands you, God the Son commands you, God the Holy Spirit commands you. The sacrament of the cross commands you. The faith of the holy apostles Peter and Paul and the other saints commands you. The blood of the martyrs commands you. The self-control of the confessors commands you. The pious intercession of all saints commands you. The power of the Christian mystery of faith commands you. So begone you trespasser of the commandments. Begone you tempter full of cunning and deceit, you the enemy of virtue, you the persecutor of the innocent. Yield, you the most atrocious, yield to Christ in whom you have found none of your works..."

Currently the Catholic Church no longer confronts exorcism in a consistently positive way. In the course of church and above all theological history, new and also critical doctrines emerged. In the mid 1970's the professor for the Old Testament in Tübingen, Professor Haag, made a talking point in his works "Farewell to the devil" and "Belief in the devil" since he held the reality of the devil to be not compulsory for Christians. Haag commented on the topic of spirit possession in "Belief in the devil" as follows: "Possession is thus a historical illness, just as its primary form of expression, hysteria, is to be understood as an era-specific conflict reaction. The function of the exorcist has been taken over today by the psychotherapist." (Haag, 1974 p. 439). And Haag wrote in the biggest German daily newspaper on 07/25/1976, with reference to the well-known case of Anneliese Michel: "Humbug! In cases of alleged spirit possession it is 90% a matter of hysteria and epilepsy. The rest are simply mental illnesses" (Bild am Sonntag, 1976).

In total contrast was the opinion of the Jesuit priest, Dr. Rodewyk, who not only wrote a paragraph in the "Lexicon for Theology and Church" about spirit possession, but who also wrote the official assessment of the case of Anneliese Michel for the Bishop of Würzburg. This assessment led to the carrying out of the major exorcism on the student from Klingenberg. On 14th August 1976, Rodewyk delivered the following statement in an interview: "The Catholic Church adheres to the belief that God created an invisible world as well as a visible world. Originally all spirits were good. Then came the Fall about which we know practically nothing in detail. Hence there is now a great host of good spirits and also one of evil spirits. Every Catholic is obliged to believe this" (Stuttgarter Nachrichten, August 1976).

A further popular Catholic theologian, Karl Rahner, writes in the "Lexicon for Theology and Church": "For a sober evaluation of spirit possession and to avoid rationalistic criticism, one should not forget that every phenomenon which is observed (similar to visions, for example) is already a synthesis of, on the one hand, demonic influence and on the other hand the perception and imagination world of an individual or of a time, abilities, illness possibilities and even of parapsychological skills. An adequate separation is essentially neither necessary nor possible. Wanting to bring conditions and experiences such as prophetic inspiration or mystical ecstasy (where these are genuine) directly into connection in a religious historical way with spirit possession misjudges the essential difference that spirit possession has a destructive effect upon a person, whereas mystical and prophetic experiences are directed to the spiritual core of a free person if they are perceived as an inescapable superior and divine power" (Rahner, 1958).

To conclude, the Catholic theologian and dogmatist, Michael Schmaus should be mentioned, who writes in his Dogmatics II/I: "But that there is a world where illness and misery reign, this comes from Satan's seduction. His rule over mankind reaches a climax in possession". (Schmaus, p. 308).

This theological tension continues in the biggest church denomination in the world. No other denomination has such a traditional and detailed description regarding exorcism. But one can also presume here that the practice of exorcism occurs more often in South America, Africa and Asia than in the USA and Western Europe.

4.3.2 Charismatic Movement within the Roman Catholic Church

As regards the charismatic movement within the Catholic Church, parallels can be found to the charismatic movement within the Protestant Church. Charismatic religiosity styles have also reached the Catholic Church, not only worldwide, but also in Europe and in Germany.

Currently the charismatic renewal of the Catholic Church in Germany is promoting among other things "Pentecost 21" on its website, a congress of the charismatic movement in Germany. Promotion includes a quotation from Pope Francis "Let's pray every day to the Holy Spirit and then the Holy Spirit will bring us closer to Christ". Here the following figures are disclosed: There are 12,000 Catholics in Germany who class themselves as part of the Catholic charismatic movement, worldwide there are said to be over 120 million Catholic charismatics. As well as the traditional Catholic teachings, elements such as worship, praise, gifts of the Spirit, healing, miracles etc. are implemented in the style of religiosity. Concerning the topic of deliverance, it is less the approach of the "Rituale Romanum" and instead more the practical approaches of the charismatic deliverance ministry.[44]

4.4 Theological Theories of Spirit Possession in Free Churches in Germany

The church landscape in Germany differs from that in other countries. There are two large churches, the Roman Catholic Church and the Protestant Church. Both are also called national churches and recruit their members through baptism. As a rule, infants are sprinkled with water in a christening ceremony at the request of their parents and so become members of theses churches. In the Protestant Church the baptism received as an infant is confirmed at the age of 14 by the act of confirmation and the confirmands are allowed to participate in communion. The situation is similar in the Catholic Church with confirmation and communion. Therefore,

44 Reference to this has already been made in Chapter 4.2.2.

in both churches infant baptism qualifies as admission into the church. As soon as these members earn their own wages, church tax[45] is deducted from these. The effect of this is that currently around 60% of the population are church members (covering both national churches) and these also pay church tax, however less than 10% of these members attend church services on Sundays. Churches are playing an increasingly smaller role in Germany. Around 1000 church members are thus daily leaving the church in Germany. This is the reason why the number of people who have no affiliation to a religion has greatly increased over the last few years. The following statistics show the development of how members were leaving the church in Germany from 1992–2013.

Figure 2: Numbers of members of leaving the Protestant and Catholic Church from 1994 to 2013[46]

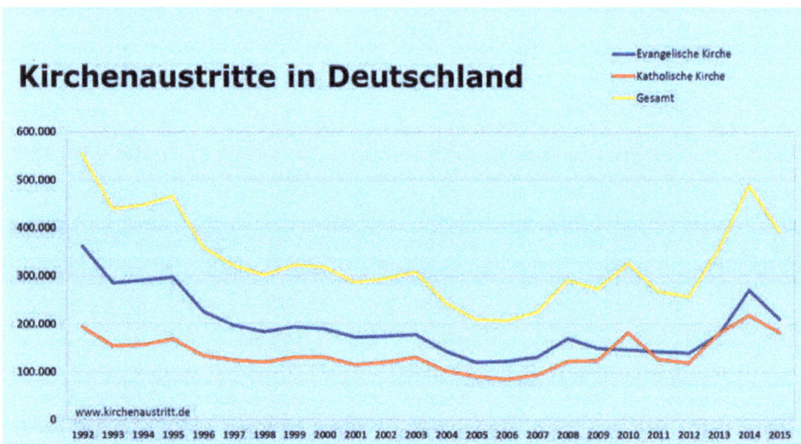

In Germany, the situation is different to that in many countries of the world where it is normal to have no difference between national and free churches. Free churches and the number of their members are a tiny amount compared to both the large churches. In 2014, 60% of the German population were members of a national church whereas only 1% were members of a

45 The church tax amounts to approx. 8–9% of the income tax, with the latter being dependent on the amount of monthly income.
46 http://www.kirchenaustritt.de/statistik 10/20/2015.

free church. However, it is currently the free churches which are growing when compared with the national churches.

Free churches are not supported by the state or by taxes, rather they are self-financing from member donations. Numbers vary considerably concerning the size of a free church. There are free churches with 20 members and others with over 1,000 members. One becomes a member of a free church by baptism.[47] The free church landscape in Germany is heterogeneous, i.e. there are a large number of free churches which are either totally independent of each other or are in free church organisations. The "Vereinigung evangelischer Freikirchen" (VEF) (Alliance of Protestant Free Churches) is a loose affiliation of free churches in Germany.[48] Currently there are 12 free churches as members in the alliance and 2 free churches are guest members. In order to provide an overview, three free church alliances and their theories on spirit possession will be presented in this thesis.

4.4.1 Bund evangelisch-freikirchlicher Gemeinden (BEFG) – Baptist Churches

The "Der Bund evangelisch-freikirchlicher Gemeinden" (Alliance of Protestant Free Churches) is the largest free church in Germany with over approx. 860 churches. The alliance is a member of the Baptist World Alliance which was founded in 1905 and is represented in 200 countries. It has more than 43 million members and 100 million churchgoers. Since this free church fosters a congregationalist church understanding (autonomy of the local congregations), it is therefore very diverse, also in doctrinal questions. Therefore, there is no unified teaching approach to questions on matters such as spirit possession und mental illness. Nevertheless, prospective pastors at the theological college in Elstal/Berlin have to attend lectures about

47 In free churches infants are not baptised, rather believing Christians according to their confession of faith in Jesus Christ. One speaks of "born again Christians".

48 Protestant Free churches do not differ from other churches due to a special teaching. They are characterised above all by a specific understanding of church and congregation as well as by their style of religiosity. Particular objectives are a free and personal decision for faith in Jesus Christ and a life committed to following Him. The free churches represent legally and organisationally the principle of self-financing and self-administration towards the state and forgo taxation. http://www.vef.de/wer-wir-sind/ 10/01/2015.

counselling and psychology in the area of practical theology. However, the topic of spirit possession is not intensively dealt with in this regard.

4.4.2 Bund freier-evangelischer Gemeinden (BFEG) – Alliance of Free Protestant Churches

The Free Protestant Churches in Germany have around 480 churches in Germany. In their theological college a lecture on "Theology and theory of counselling" is offered in the 5th semester. The students learn here about the distinction between counselling and theology and how various counselling concepts are theologically established. Additionally, a seminar on the topic of "Introduction to holistic counselling" takes place every three weeks.[49]

4.4.3 Bund freikirchlicher Pfingstgemeinden (BFP) – Alliance of Pentecostal Churches

The Alliance of Pentecostal Churches in Germany and its 700 churches or more belongs to the world Pentecostal movement.[50] Compared to the other free churches in Germany and due to its historical development, it is closer to having a theological concept when it comes to spirit possession. The reason for this is found in the history of the Pentecostal movement which is indeed still very young (barely 100 years old), but which relates strongly to the supernatural aspects of Christianity, where the belief in Satan, demons etc. is to be reckoned with.

In 2006, the following explanation was given by the president and the deputy of the "Alliance of Pentecostal Churches" (BFP) at a pastors' convention:

---

49 http://th-ewersbach.de/fuenfjaehriges-studium-bama/praktische-theologie.html 10/02/1015.

50 The Pentecostal movement denotes a diversity of Christian groups which embody in the broadest sense "enthusiastic Christianity". What they have in common in their teaching, though the views are often very contrasting, is to experience the particular working of the Holy Spirit in the end times. Speaking in tongues is for most groups a necessary sign of a special equipping with the Holy Spirit (baptism in the Spirit).

1. As biblical Christians we believe that people can be demonised and have a need for deliverance ministry. This ministry of deliverance can clearly be seen in the ministry of our Lord Jesus Christ as well as in the ministry of his apostles.
2. Jesus does not leave us alone as a church with the task of deliverance, rather He gives us clear guidelines through His word as to how we are to manage this task. No-one needs to be uncertain here and every 'new' teaching on this or that topic has to be measured against His word. If we find a teaching in the Bible then we call it biblical; if we don't find it then we rate it as un-biblical. We know that we are obligated to the Holy Scripture also for this topic. "All Scripture is God-breathed and is useful for teaching, rebuking, correcting and training in righteousness" (2 Tim 3:16). 'What you heard from me, keep as the pattern of sound teaching' (2 Tim 1:13).
3. As well as biblical teaching there is also of course the area of personal, individual leading of the Holy Spirit in the methods we use. For example, the normal biblical way for ministering to people who are ill consists of the laying on of hands and/or anointing with oil (Mark 16:18/James 5:14). Despite this we read how Jesus in one case smeared mud on the eyes of a blind man and asked him to wash himself and this led to his healing (John 9). The Bible thus teaches (normative) a clear way and at the same time describes (descriptive) how those ministering can be individually led to apply various methods beneficially. Therefore, we can have plenty of freedom in following the guidance of the Spirit and to be sensitive to this leading. This also applies to the area of deliverance ministry. However, it is imperative to heed this: even good experiences should never be formulated nor judged as a teaching. Whoever cannot distinguish clearly here leaves serious biblical-theological ground behind and opens themselves to subjective influences.
4. The New Testament clearly describes the deliverance ministry of Jesus and the apostles in the context of their missionary ministry. In the apostolic letters to the churches the notion of the battle "flesh against spirit" and of healing is clearly at the centre, and a deliverance ministry for Christians is not recommended anywhere. On the contrary we are advised as Christians to concentrate our faith on Christ...that Christ will dwell in our hearts by faith, so that we will be rooted and established in love... (Eph 3:17). Therefore, we do not believe either that it can be normal for God's children to have

to struggle with being bound by demonic powers. That this sanctification in Christ is a clear goal for every Christian is mentioned in Jesus' quality description: "So if the Son sets you free, you will be free indeed" (John 8:36) This is the reason that Paul says to the Christians in Corinth: "...I do not want you to be participants with demons. You cannot drink the cup of the Lord and of demons too; you cannot have a part in both the Lord's table and the table of demons" (1.Cor 10:20–21). Repentance is the biblical way to get rid of demons. For example: "Therefore each of you must put off falsehood and speak truthfully with his neighbour, for we are all members of one body" (Eph 4:25). The instruction is not to drive out a spirit of lies, rather to seize the authority in Christ and to put this faith into action.
5. The main aim of demons is to weaken our faith in Christ. "The Spirit however clearly says that in later times some will abandon the faith and follow deceiving spirits and things taught by demons" (1 Tim 4:1). Therefore, we fully concentrate on strengthening people in this faith that Christ is almighty. Should a Christian nevertheless be evidently demonised for whatever reason, then we recommend deliverance ministry according to the example set in biblical teaching.

Uwe Schäfer / Ingolf Ellßel
Erzhausen, 06/01/2006.

For pastors it has become clear in recent years that in their theological training there is a prominent deficit in knowledge in the areas of counselling, spirit possession und mental illness. For this reason, the training of future Pentecostal pastors was improved in this respect. Since 2014, all students at the Theological College of Beröa have been taught about an introduction to counselling[51] in 18 double lessons and about counselling practice[52] in a further 18 double hours. In a third block of 18 double hours the students are also taught about:

- Counselling and psychology/psychotherapy in dialogue
- Principles and insight into various therapy approaches
- Competence limitations of the counsellor

51 http://www.beroea.info/images/beroea/pdf/studienhandbuch_2015-2016.pdf 10/03/2015.

52 http://www.beroea.info/images/beroea/pdf/studienhandbuch_2015-2016.pdf 10/03/2015.

- Pastoral "first aid" up until therapeutic treatment
- Classification of various disorders with the aid of ICD-10
- Pastoral treatment possibilities e.g. with depression and anxiety disorders.

In the third year of study they additionally visit a psychiatric clinic[53] and once a year a training day in the area of counselling takes place where specialists are invited to give lectures on counselling topics.

To summarise one could say that the free church movement has become aware of the increasing psychic needs in society and is striving to find answers for people's questions. There is an attempt to account for these insights in recent years by incorporating counselling and psychological knowledge into the training concepts for future pastors. The area of spirit possession und mental illness is not explicitly dealt with, but is nevertheless addressed.

In this thesis the work and understanding of free church pastors has been specifically included as well as literature research and the explanation of what psychology and theology teach about the topic of spirit possession, the historical outline and the cultural backgrounds.

Thus theoretical knowledge can be linked to the current and practical experiences of pastors. In this way, essential conclusions and discussion approaches emerge which should present a gain in knowledge for psychology in exactly this specialised area. And possibly through this an individual free church pastor or also free church organisations can be helped.

How exactly the methodology was applied in this research project will now be explained in the following chapter.

53 https://www.hohemark.de/startseite/ 10/03/2015.

5 Methodology

This study focused on exploring the perceptions of free church pastors' perceptions of spirit possession and mental illness. The number of German individuals who frequent pastors with symptoms that could be described within the psychological framework as a mental illness is growing. While these symptoms may be diagnosed within the framework of psychology as a mental illness, the reality is that these patients believe that their experiences are linked more so towards spirit possession and pastors approached may be placed in a position where the nature of their training may guide the treatment plan pursued. As such, it is necessary to understand how free church pastors in Germany perceive spirit possession and mental illnesses. In lieu of this, the chapter outlines the methodology chosen for the current study, which is the qualitative paradigm. The decision for the qualitative interviews will be discussed alongside the research questions and the structure of the interviews with the free church pastors. In addition, the sample will be described and the analytical tool utilised discussed.

5.1 Research objective

This research project aimed to explore the perceptions of mental illness and spirit possession amongst free church pastors in Germany. Free church pastors often find themselves working with individuals who present symptoms that are believed to be spirit possession. However, upon investigation, the symptoms of spirit possession are remarkably similar to those which characterise mental illnesses, for example schizophrenia, where the patient hears voices and has a deluded sense of reality, or depression, where the patient becomes withdrawn. Or, in the case of bipolar disorder where the patient experiences drastic shifts in mood and affect, the patient may be perceived as experiencing a spirit possession. Through investigating the perceptions of spirit possession and mental illness held by free church pastors, this research aims to provide a deeper understanding of the complexity of the situation that is faced by free church pastors, who may require additional psychological training. Thus, the research project aims to explore the experience of spirit possession and mental illnesses and to investigate whether pastors are able to appropriately diagnose a client, given the similarity in symptoms and expression. This understanding is essential, given that patients may be receiving inappropriate treatment for the symptoms they show. The research objective is generally to establish and explain the current position of psychological and theological explanations and understanding on the topic of spirit possession from an international as well as national (German) perspective. Specifically the project hones in on free church pastors in Germany and how they specifically attend to those seeking advice in this context. The benefit of this understanding is that it will aid the development of an understanding between the DSM-5 categorisation and definitions of the spirit possession from the perspective of the pastors. This becomes integral to the appropriate and relevant treatment being rendered, since if misdiagnosed, the symptoms may manifest in more serious consequences.

5.2 Rationale

A review of the literature provided an understanding that a major focus has been placed on spirit possession from the perspectives of the patient. There is a growing need however to locate understanding and research from the perspective of the practitioners, be they faith healers, traditional healers or pastors. This perspective becomes integral, especially for the appropriate treatment of patients. Given that pastors may not have the appropriate understanding of mental illness, not being equipped with the appropriate education to effectively distinguish between mental illnesses and spirit possession, this exploration is vital. In Germany, other than the publication of books by Kurt Koch in the 1950's, there has been no real assistance for pastors and specifically for how they deal with patients in this context. Depending on the church denomination, one is quick to employ the so-called deliverance ministry in order to "drive demons out" of the inflicted person. This is the case throughout the Pentecostal-charismatic area of Christianity, which nevertheless includes approximately 500 million people worldwide; it is a Protestant movement which propagates healings, signs and wonders and likewise the deliverance from demonic powers. This is how pastors in Pentecostal-charismatic churches proceed, not only worldwide, but specifically in Germany. Other pastors are uncertain when it comes to possession and describe this as "medieval" and assume a case of mental illness (schizophrenia, delirium or a personality disorder). However, what they all have in common is that they require information and specialised knowledge in this area, since theological studies do not convey appropriate psychological knowledge.

This thesis attempts to bridge the gap between theology and psychology by exploring the perceptions of free church pastors in Germany. It is the opinion of the researcher that this understanding will be able to be developed as an effective tool for counselling those seeking advice in this special context.

5.3 Design/Approach

Broadly, this research is located within the qualitative tradition. Qualitative research might mean different things in different fields but a generic definition is given by Denzin & Lincoln (2003). They state that "qualitative research is a situated activity that locates the observer in the world. It consists of a set of interpretive, material practices that makes the world visible. These practices transform the world. They turn the world into a series of representations ... Qualitative researchers study things in their natural settings, attempting to make sense of, or to interpret, phenomena in terms of the meanings people bring to them" (Denzin & Lincoln, 2003, p. 4–5). In light of the aims of the study, which is to explore perceptions of spirit possession and mental illness amongst free church pastors, the qualitative approach was deemed most appropriate as it would allow the researcher to engage with participants in their natural setting and would allow for depth of understanding to occur.

We have to take cognizance of the multiple and varied subjective experiences and interpretations of reality (Guba and Lincoln, 1994; Kvalem & Brinkmann, 2009). Individuals' interpretations of their social world are largely informed by the different meanings that they give to events and experiences. Furthermore, individuals give meaning to as well as draw meaning from these events and experiences (Krauss, 2005) and therefore are engaged in a continuous dynamic and active relation to the social world. A qualitative research approach allows us to understand and explore these dialectic processes of meaning and interpretation (Kelly, 1999).

According to Mertens (2005) there are three possible inter-related reasons for choosing a qualitative method of research: the researcher's view of the world; the nature of the research questions; and practical reasons associated with the nature of qualitative methods. A fourth reason may be that the original data are best described as "thick", an adjective used by Midgley (2004) to differentiate semi-structured interviews, for example, from closed questionnaires. All four reasons inform both aspects of the research. As Denzin and Lincoln observe, the word "qualitative" implies an emphasis on "the qualities of entities and on processes and meanings" (Denzin & Lincoln, 2003, p. 13). Such qualities include the capturing of information that is only made possible by getting close to experience, particularly individual subjectivity. Midgley (2004) proposes a useful definition of qualitative research by indicating what it does not propose to do: Qualitative research is an approach that aims less at prediction and statistical correlation, and more at discovery and increased understanding of the human world (Midgley, 2004, p. 92).

5.3.1 Main characteristics on qualitative research

According to Flick (2006), qualitative research has three main characteristics:

A) Object appropriateness of methods and theories (in the case of demonic possession and which concepts free church pastors have, this is the object to be taken into account, and as such the point of reference for the choice of the methods and not vice-versa).
B) Consideration and analysis of the most different perspectives (the varying and subjective perspectives of the individual pastors and their respective concepts can thus be effectively taken into account).
C) The reflexivity of the researcher and their research (all observations, perceptions, emotions and impressions from the interviews will be taken into account and will become data that will likewise flow into the research results).

Since statements of free church pastors are being dealt with, it was important to collect the various subjective perspectives of the interview partners and to compare them in order to draw conclusions to construct a theory. All information from the pastors can be collected, classified and interpreted independently of each other. The particular personal reports stay completely preserved in form and content. The neutral attitude of the interviewer does not influence this form of information search. The methodological approach in this thesis is specifically about collecting particular information from 11 free church pastors by the use of interviews and to compare[54] them in order to develop a reasonable theory.

Graphically, it could be illustrated like this:

Figure 3: Model of sampling and data collection[55]

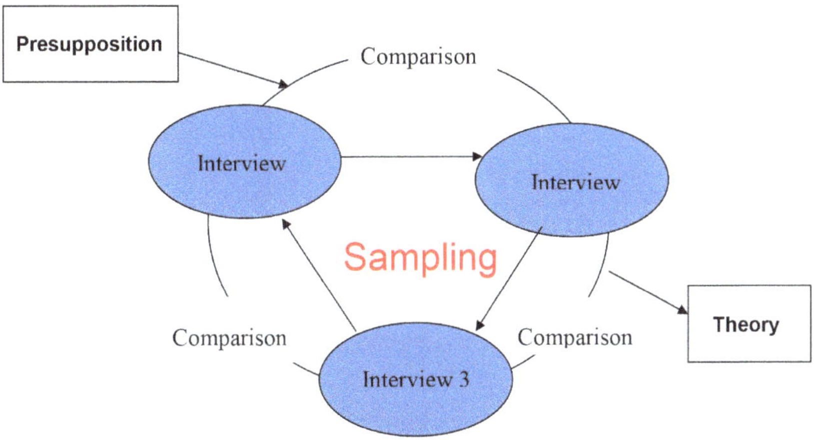

5.3.2 Interviews

Of the many materials used in qualitative research, Denzin and Lincoln (2003) list interviews as an effective tool. If an interview is performed based on a specified "standardised questionnaire" (in which the same questions in the same formulation and sequence are available to all respondents) and by an interviewer who adheres exactly to these guidelines, it is called a survey in a "strongly structured interview situation". Standardisation and extensive neutrality of the interviewer as transmitter of questions are accordingly the most important differentiating factors of this form of interview in relation to the above-mentioned ones. The interview of individuals (here of free church pastors) under these conditions represents the major form of investigation in the

54 The individual key aspects and conclusions are illustrated by means of tables (Chapter 5.5).

55 Own developed model.

empirical social research (Schnell, Hill & Esser, p. 322–323). In standardised interviews, each respondent is asked the same questions and this is how an equality of the interview situation is achieved. The questions are in fact the same, but the answers are different. This is intentional, because in this way all respondents always receive the same guidelines of interpretation for their answer. If the question changes, it can no longer be decided whether differences in the answers that occur between the respondents are to be traced back to differences in the method of measurement or to actual differences between the characteristics that are to be measured (Maccoby & Maccoby 1965, p. 40). In addition, an absolute neutrality of the interviewer is essential, towards both the respondent and the subject. "In his reactions, the interviewer must keep himself within a tight limit – it is even a basic principle of each questionnaire that the interviewer must try to hide his own attitude on the object of investigation. He also must not show surprise or disapproval about anything that the respondent says, nor should he nod enthusiastically when the respondent expresses the own attitude of the interviewer. It has turned out to be an effective compromise that the interviewer adopts an attitude of friendly connivance" (Maccoby & Maccoby 1965 p. 63).

5.3.3 Research Questions

The following questions guided the interview with the participants:

A) Do free church pastors understand the difference between mental illness and demon possession?
B) If a patient is diagnosed with a mental illness, how does the free church pastor proceed?
C) If a patient is diagnosed as being possessed by a demon, how does the free church pastor proceed?

These questions will enable the framing of the interviews with free church pastors and will allow the researcher the opportunity to gather information that will aid in the development of a framework that can be used by free church pastors to better understand, differentiate and treat patients who show either a mental illness or who are believed to be possessed. This is integral to the well-being of patients as a misdiagnosis may precipitate symptoms further.

5.3.4 Interview guide

The sensitive nature of the subject matter requires some strategy on the part of the researcher. The following interview guide enabled the researcher to remain within the framework that is set for the study:

- Introduction (I will introduce myself and the research project, point out that the interview will be recorded and that data protection regulations are involved, thank the person for their willingness to support my research project by participating in the interview)
- Questions on age, marital status, school qualifications, years in the profession, denomination will be asked
- Questions on theological training/study (length, qualification)
- Questions on concepts and foreknowledge of the subject of possession and mental illness
- Questions on experience of this subject in day to day life as a pastor
- Questions on a specific case study[56]
- Questions about schizophrenia
- Questions on the evaluation of their own competence in the area of possession and mental illness[57]

5.4 Sampling

As far as "sampling" is concerned in qualitative research, there is a focus on the richness of the information (Fossey, Harvey, McDermott & Davidson, 2002). This pursuit of "rich" information informed the selection of participants in this study. In terms of the data corpus, there are two broad populations from which participants were selected. Pastors from free churches in Germany were selected for participation. This selection of participants can be described as purposive (Fossey et al., 2002). The interviews were carried out with 11 free church pastors who have been in full-time service for at least ten years, who represent different free church denominations and are of both sexes.

56 See Appendix for the case study.
57 See Appendix for interview schedule.

5.5 Participant demographics

Pastors from various free churches in Germany and two in Africa[58] were conducted and were asked if they were prepared to be interviewed for the purposes of this research project. This was undertaken by telephone and email. Out of 20 pastors who were approached, 11 gave consent to participate in the study. Appointments were made with the 11 pastors and the interviews were carried out and recorded at a time and place that was suitable to the participant.

The demographics of the 11 participants can be summarizsd as follows:

Pastor	Country	Gender	Age	Pastor since...years	Denomination	Treated Spirit Possession
1	Germany	M	38	10	Baptist	No
2	Germany	M	42	10	Baptist	No
3	Germany	M	47	10	Free evangelical	No
4	Germany	M	42	11	Pentecostal	No
5	Germany	F	41	14	Free evangelical	No
6	Germany	M	50	20	Charismatic	Yes
7	Germany	M	43	11	Pentecostal	No
8	Germany	M	37	10	Pentecostal	No
9	Germany	M	55	25	Baptist	No
10	Uganda	M	58	20	Charismatic	Yes
11	Tanzania	M	67	30	Baptist	Yes

Description

In total, 11 free church pastors were interviewed. 9 of the pastors were from Germany and this was deemed a suitable number given that the aim of the study was not to draw large conclusions regarding the area of spirit possession. Rather, the aim was to explore the perceptions of spirit possession and mental illness that were held and how this understanding can be utilised to aid in the development of a framework that will allow for the appropriate

58 The author was in Uganda and Tanzania from 06/14/2015-06/29/2015 and gained insight into the deliverance ministry of a Baptist church and a charismatic church.

diagnosis of patients, be it spirit possession or mental illness. On a field trip to Africa in 2015, the researcher travelled to Uganda and Tanzania to observe and interview two pastors. These interviews are included, as these pastors are free church pastors. The author is aware of the contextual difference between Germany and Africa, but decided that including the interviews would not affect the results as the pastors from free church denominations hold the same ideology, regardless of geographic location. Of the eleven participants, ten were male and one was female. This gender skew is based on a tradition that has seen more men than women being allowed the opportunity to train as a pastor. Given that the study does not particularly focus on gender issues, this was not considered problematic. The age of the participants ranged between 38 years and 70 years. All the participants had between ten years and 30 years of professional experience as free church pastors. Indicative from this, is that the participants can be said to hold concrete understandings of the functioning of the free church ministry. Specifically, participants were from four different churches.

5.6 Data collection using the semi-structured interviews

Semi-structured interviews were used to collect data from free church pastors. The advantages of interview-based data collection are that it allows the researcher to get a full range and depth of information, to develop a relationship with the participant that supports data collection, and it promotes flexibility (Mertens, 2005). Eleven participants were interviewed. The time and venue for the individual interviews were determined by the participants and all individual interviewees requested that they be interviewed at their place of work. This facilitated a discussion of work-related experiences because interviewees literally responded from a professional perspective. The 11 person-to-person interviews ranged in duration from 45 to 90 minutes. Each interview began with an expression of gratitude for agreeing to participate in the research and for giving up time to be interviewed. Each interviewee was presented with two forms that required their signature; the research participation consent form and the audio-recording consent form (see Appendix I). An identical interview schedule (see Appendix II) provided the basis for all the interviews) and interviewees received a copy.

The interview schedule consisted of 16 questions that guided the gathering of data and addressed the research questions. The questions were formulated in part as a result of the information that emerged from the literature review, in part as a result of personal knowledge and engagement with the experiences of spirit possession. Given the nature of the enquiry it was felt that the "voices" of the interview participants needed to be clear. The format of the interview was semi-structured with the schedule serving as a suggested guide to the discussion rather than a directive in terms of questions and responses. There was opportunity for dialogic interaction, particularly in relation to ideas for possible future developments in the field, but it was gathering the interviewees' experiences of working within the area of spirit possession that was foregrounded.

5.7 Thematic content analysis

In light of the research objectives for the project, thematic content analysis was selected as the appropriate analytical tool as it allowed the researcher to thematise, categorise and analyse the data obtained. Thematic content analysis can be understood to be an interpretative application of content analysis in which the focus of analysis is on thematic content that is identified, categorised and elaborated on the basis of systematic scrutiny (Banister, Burman, Parker, Taylor & Tindall, 1994). According to Lieblich, Tuval-Mashiach and Zilber (1998), thematic content analysis is one of the various ways of analysing narrative material. It enables scholars, observers or practitioners to use a wide variety of information in a systematic manner. Thematic content analysis is a qualitative analytic method for "identifying, analyzing and reporting patterns (themes) within data. It minimally organizes and describes your data set in (rich) detail" (Braun & Clarke, 2006, p. 79). The current research was not located in deeper nuances that may have been allowed, if discourse analyses or narrative analysis was selected. Rather, the objective was steeped in wanting to understand how free church pastors understand the interaction between mental illness and spirit possession, in light of the similarities in symptoms. However, Braun and Clark (2006) state that thematic content analysis should not be mistaken for a technique that merely describes data. Rather, they state "it goes further than this, and interprets various aspects of the research topic"

(p. 79). Furthermore, thematic analysis requires more involvement and interpretation from the researcher. As a technique, it moves beyond counting and explicit ideas within the data, that is, themes. Themes may be initially generated inductively from the raw information, or generated deductively from theory and prior research (Boyatzis, 1998). Coffey and Atkinson (1996, p. 27) state that, "coding can be thought about as a way of relating our data to our ideas about these data." Krippendorf (1980) outlined the principles guiding the categorisation of data for content analysis in terms of the purposes for defining the data and the process needed for defining the data. Eagle (1998) explains that this could be understood as asking "why", "what" and "how" questions of data analysis. She further argues that there is little discussion of the epistemological basis of content analysis in texts about the methodology, and that it appears that data categories can be both theoretically and empirically derived. Thus, some categorisation may be a priori, while others may be generated within the process of data analysis (Eagle, 1998). According to Braun and Clarke (2006), thematic content analysis involves six steps. The first step involves the reading and transcribing of the data. Secondly, initial codes were generated and thereafter codes were assembled into potential themes. The fourth step entailed the generation of a thematic map. The fifth step required each theme to be defined and named. The final step was the production of a report (Braun & Clarke, 2006). These steps were followed in analysis of the data. Thematic content analysis is the method most suited to the aims of this research study, which involved eliciting and analysing the narratives of free church pastors in the context of spirit possession.

6 Results and Discussion

This thesis examined the perception of free church pastors in Germany regarding their understanding of spirit possession and mental illness. The aim was to explore the perceptions held, specifically as they apply in relation to their working with patients, who present symptoms that are diagnosable either as spirit possession or mental illness. In light of the similarity of symptoms between the two experiences, this understanding is essential as misdiagnosis may influence the treatment trajectory of the patient.

The thematic content analysis enabled the identification of four themes. These are 1) distinction between spirit possession and mental illness; 2) understanding and treatment of mental illness; 3) understanding and treatment of spirit possession and 4) framework. In the sections that follow, each theme will be discussed.

6.1 Theme 1: Distinction between mental illness and spirit possession

The field of psychology has placed much emphasis on the biological and psychological aspects of the causes and manifestations of psychological disturbances (Ally, 2009). The Diagnostic and Statistical Manual of Mental Disorders adds that regardless of the original cause of mental illness, it must be considered a manifestation of a behavioural, psychological or biological dysfunction. According to Ally (2009), definitions like this permeate the field of psychopathology, and even though they address many of the aspects related to the manifestation of psychological disturbances, they are limited in some respects. One major limitation is the non-inclusion of the possible influence of spiritual beliefs in the origin of mental illness. Belief in possession by spirits is common in many cultures, both Western and non-Western (Stafford, 2005). Evil spirits are defined as "...more or less intelligent beings which with a will of their own, seem to bother or oppress us, or in rare instances, possess our bodies" (Stafford, 2005, p. 14). Individuals experiencing themselves to be possessed by these spirits sometimes show supernatural strength and agility or behave self-destructively. Other signs include rolling eyes, fetid smells and screams (Stafford, 2005). Further symptoms include changes to the personality, physique and the voice of the possessed (Dwyer, 2003). It is also reported by McNutt (1995) that an individual who has recovered from a possession experience will not remember his or her actions during that period. One can thus say that the experience of spirit possession is similar to physical and psychological states that indicate out-of-the ordinary experiences or altered states of consciousness.

To a Western psychologist, the symptoms of spirit possession outlined above may point to a specific mental illness, while in many other societies these symptoms are taken as evidence of the influence of some spiritual entity.

The distinction between mental illness and spirit possession in the literature has not been clearly delineated, given that the symptoms of the two experiences are so similar.

Furthermore, Rogo (1974) indicated that spirit possession is an experience that exists in most cultures and religions. In fact, in the earliest of civilisations, Greek mythology indicates that insanity was sent by the Gods (Plato, 427–347 BC). The person afflicted start behaving in strange and atypical ways. The person possessed can become violent, speak with a different voice and suddenly know a new language (Ellenberger, 1970). However, psychologically speaking, the discipline does not readily accept that a person can be possessed by spirits, unless this is viewed as a manifestation of symptoms from a mental illness, like schizophrenia, for example.

In light of the conflicting viewpoints within the discipline of psychology regarding spirit possession, one can only begin to imagine the complexity faced outside of the field. For example, by a pastor whose duties include not only ministerial work, but also counselling of individuals who belong to a particular church. Here, pastors are faced with individuals who present symptoms that are diagnosable under the umbrella of psychology as a mental illness, requiring psychological intervention. However, these same patients, when confronting the pastor are more likely to be viewed from within the paradigm of the church and a diagnosis of spirit possession is assumed.

In this respect, the participants' understanding of the distinction between mental illness and spirit possession was of particular interest to the researcher. Participant 1 indicated: *That's a difficult question. Personally I've had no experience of that. I see it in the biblical testimonies. I think it can seem the same or similar to schizophrenia, with peculiar behaviour and perceptions. But actually I have no personal experience of it.* Despite not having the experience of working with spirit possession per se, the participant alludes to the overlap of symptoms. Participant 7 provided a very interesting notion, one that almost excluded possession from biblical texts: *Spirit possession isn't found in the Bible, as far as I would judge. A Christian cannot be possessed.* This was an interesting notion, given that literature indicates that spirit possession is mentioned in various verses and biblical texts (for example: Matthew 8:28; 12:28; Mark 5:5, 16:17, Luke 8:27; Ephesians 6:11–12).

However, as the participant shared more, he stated: *I don't know to what extent this goes if a person has made a pact with Satan. The Bible speaks more about people being demonised and that is where I see chances for deliverance ministry to expel demons. From my point of view it doesn't have to proceed as Derek Prince described it, with loud screaming as the demons are expelled. You can also bind and expel demons silently. We have been given authority and so this is possible. It doesn't always have to have the effects that others describe.* Based on this participant's experience and understanding, a spirit possession may not occur in the drastic descriptions that it has become synonymous with. Rather, he suggests, that the spirit may not present itself in explosive ways. Regardless, a developing narrative, suggesting that pastors may find it difficult in distinguishing between a mental illness and spirit possession state, started to emerge.

Participant 8 said that it is "*Not so easy to describe, but when people express things and when certain things manifest themselves which on the one hand cannot be explained by human understanding and which are furthermore a strong expression of what can be perceived as evil or what can be understood as evil.*" He stated further "*Maybe one distinctive feature of possession is a sort of compulsion towards self-destruction. Like the boy who kept throwing himself into the fire in the Bible, that people harm themselves, so a lifestyle that consistently harms them, but also harms others as a consequence, a form of expression that is strongly destructive.*" Adding to this description of spirit possession, participant 6 said that "*usually people will come with strong deficiencies in some areas. Some are strong emotional eruptions like uncontrollable anger, uncontrollable fears, uncontrollable lust and they are dominated by those emotions and although they have tried to escape, they come to a point where they realise that they are captive, like an addicted person. So they seek help. I would say that most of them at the moment when they start seeking help are not aware of the combination of psychological personality problems that they have and the evil spirit that strengthens the problems they have."*

It becomes evident that despite the majority of the participants not working with spirit possession, they understand its expression to represent the manifestation of physical and psychological symptoms that are attributed to an outside force or spirit that enters the body and takes control over the person's mind, behaviour and emotions. In fact, it can be taken as far as stating that all participants in this study had an understanding of spirit possession that was akin to that found in the literature (Jehl, 2005; O'Grady, 1989) as well as biblical texts (for example: Matthew 8:28; 12:28; Mark 5:5, 16:17, Luke 8:27; Ephesians 6:11–12).

In exploring the distinction between mental illness and spirit possession, the participants were provided with a case-study. The case-study itself was taken from a psychology textbook and clearly presents a patient with symptoms that are indicative of a mental illness.

Participant responses to the case study depicting mental illness:

Pastor	Country	Denomination	Treated Spirit Possession	Case study Spirit Possessed, Mental Illness, not sure?
1	Germany	Baptist	No	Mental Illness
2	Germany	Baptist	No	Mental Illness
3	Germany	Free evangelical	No	Mental Illness
4	Germany	Pentecostal	No	Not sure
5	Germany	Free evangelical	No	Mental Illness
6	Germany	Charismatic	Yes	Spirit Possessed
7	Germany	Pentecostal	No	Not sure
8	Germany	Pentecostal	No	Not sure
9	Germany	Baptist	No	Mental Illness
10	Uganda	Charismatic	Yes	Spirit Possessed
11	Tanzania	Baptist	Yes	Spirit Possessed

6.1.1 Pastors who had treated and diagnosed spirit possession

Participants 6, 10 and 11 claimed to have dealt with spirit possession at some point in the course of their pastoral ministry. It followed, that these participants categorised the case study as reflecting spirit possession. Two were from a charismatic church (numbers 6 and 10) and one from a Baptist church (number 11). In diagnosing a person with spirit possession, participant 6 stated that: *Whether people agree or not, I am a Bible believing Christian so my world view is centred around the reality of God who is Spirit and the reality of a personal enemy whose name is Satan or the devil and if humans were created in the image of God, and have fallen from their state with God, so they needed redemption by Jesus Christ our Lord and saviour, so whatever your world view is, I'm going to explain the phenomena through a Christian viewpoint. Generally, all the work of the devil is built on lies and the Bible says that Jesus Christ has come to set us free, he said that you will receive truth, you shall recognise or comprehend or come to know or experience the truth and the truth shall set you free. So if people believe lies about themselves or about reality, they open themselves up for problems. If you believe you are ugly, that will determine a lot of things, how you view life. If your parents have always told you that you are evil or that you are incapable of managing life, your self-worth will be damaged. And it is in these damages usually that the influence of evil spirits starts to work on and seeks entrance in a human life.*

Despite the clear indication and presence of psychological experiences and social experiences that may lead towards the development of symptoms that characterise a mental illness, participant 6 was insistent that the real enemy faced by humans is Satan or the devil and that one's redemption is through prayer.

He stated further that *some of the most common problems humans have are around the issue of rejection and although obviously there is a psychic side to that, what I believe and what I view as a human person, then also God has a perfect plan and the devil has a perfectly evil plan for the human person. And sometimes mothers reject their children strongly after conception already, considering abortion for example, and sometimes it seems that even spirits of rejection can enter a person prematurely even before birth. I don't personally think that, as in the new sphere of teachings in the area of this deliverance ministry, I am not so convinced that we inherit spiritual problems; I am convinced we inherit them mostly by the behaviour of our parents or simply physically, DNA or so. Some disagree on that point, I am not too strong on it, I am looking on a pragmatic side, I don't care where the dirt comes from sometimes, I try to just help people to have a clean life where they are in control of their lives by their own willpower.*

It therefore seems that if a patient presents symptoms that may be diagnosed by a mental health practitioner as a mental illness, these may be disregarded as such by this pastor, who said that the belief in God was sufficient to guide a person towards a "clean life".

Participant 10 and participant 11 provided similar responses. For example, Participant 11 stated: *I would say that this is spirit possession. He should commit suicide. Here I would pray and command the demons to leave this person. Also he should go regularly to church, preferably to our Baptist church.* Participant 10 indicated that the case study was a clear case of possession: *that is possession. A spirit, a demon of death which is tormenting the man. It wants him to commit suicide. I would drive it out in the name of Jesus.*

It must be noted however that these pastors are from African contexts and in comparison with the other participants who were all German, only one (participant 6) provided information regarding working with spirit possession. It is possible that the country, and more importantly the context and the culture connected to it, plays a larger role than denomination affiliation itself. However, a cross-cultural comparison was not the focal point of the research project. Rather, the project sought to develop a deeper understanding of the perceptions that pastors have regarding spirit possession and mental illness and regardless of context, this understanding is imperative given that misdiagnosis may alter the treatment history of the patient.

Building on what participant 6 stated, his understanding of a mental illness is required: *Mental illness can have several roots. I am not a professor on this, but one you can have a damaged brain. I know people who have been stuck in the birth canal in their mother's womb, so they didn't have enough oxygen, so they were brain damaged. In epilepsy, even the Bible knows various types of epilepsy, some routing in a certain brain deformation. I think that in the DNA you can have something that makes you already tend towards certain things, but the main thrust of psychic illnesses comes from the way people are raised as children, definitely; how they are treated, did they have loving parents, were their parents controlling, were they allowed to develop normally, did they have guidelines, were they taught to handle life in a meaningful way, were their emotional needs met. I would say these questions determine the health of the person in the long term, more than we know.*

Even though participant 9 informed us that he does not treat patients with spirit possession, he indicated that when faced with a client whose symptoms are representative of the affliction he would *always look for therapeutic help for people like this, but I also listen as to how they interpret it spiritually. The longer I am in ministry, the more I experience how helpless the therapists sometimes are, how helpless psychologists are in their interpretation of the cases, but also in their treatment of mentally ill people. Here near our church is the "Reichenau", a peninsula, and we have a doctor from our church who is active there, but when she tells me of how she is under cost pressure and simply has to fire off the people with medication and a meaningful, very deep conversation to give advice cannot take place; when I hear that then I get angry and say that our system here is so bad, our health system. That's one thing and then on top of this that they are actually very well trained and educated therapists and psychologists, but sometimes they have little counselling experience, and experience with people. A person said to me in this church that, with a case like you told me about, that three years of therapy still hadn't helped him. That helps me and I ask myself, for heaven's sake, what had they done with him? For three years going from one health cure to the next and here a little bit and there a little bit. And I ask myself, for heaven's sake, what do they do with these patients, why don't they go in-depth with them, right into the past, uncovering words that were said to them, words that have been buried, but then to find concepts that will help them dig them up and to make them visible, like Paul says, "take captive your thoughts", hold them before you and look at them, are they right or wrong? Many people don't have this concept – for them they see a disorder and some worldly wisdom is passed on and apart from that they are given medical treatment, I find that appalling. You asked though about the overlaps, but for me that is part of it. I think that Satan can have influence as the opposing force to God and can use these phenomena to destroy a person. That is why I would always accompany treatment with prayer, but then in a simple way, a prayer is said that concerns the patient and then anointing with oil in order to place the power of Jesus upon that person and that must be enough, and then to make accessible all forms of therapeutic help, as long as they are really good, to help this person, that is how I would do it.*

There seems to be a leaning more towards biblical interpretations rather than a focus on the actual, biological, psychological and social conditions that may give rise to the symptoms presented by a patient who will then be diagnosed as being possessed by a spirit.

6.1.2 Pastors who diagnosed mental illness

Five of the eleven Free Church pastors interviewed assumed it to be a case of mental illness. Participant 5 said: *I would try and find a possibility for therapy straight away, someone the person could trust and who I knew had professional training. Spontaneously I would speak of a schizophrenic development here and the man urgently needs help, since this is dangerous. I would really spend time with him, listen to him, and take him seriously. Here I would, as a counsellor, reach my limits, even with the training that I have. I think I would understand his abnormal illness and would refer him to an appropriate therapy. It depends a lot on how he interprets the phenomenon himself, if he has integrated it into his faith and thinks that the devil is speaking to him, then I would speak to him as a theologian and say I want to take that seriously and I will pray for you for deliverance, and we don't have to do that ten times, once is enough, otherwise I wouldn't be taking Jesus seriously. Then I would anoint him with oil and then refer him on immediately to someone who could give him therapy.*

Another participant indicated that his *reaction would be that I would distinguish what my direct task would be as a pastor, why did he come to speak to me as a pastor and not go to a doctor. So to clarify my area of responsibility I would definitely pray with him and encourage him on the spiritual side and pray that these powers will have no control over him, but I wouldn't just leave him there, I would, if it was so acute, accompany him personally to a doctor, or a psychologist or psychiatrist and see that he gets treatment, perhaps medication as a treatment. I wouldn't try to play the psychologist, but rather see that he gets treatment, because it is so acute, this acute suicide drive, this voice, that this is covered and that one can begin to work on from where it comes* (Participant 1).

Despite the participant's indication of the case representing mental illness, their response alluded to the treatment plan, which slanted more towards religious-orientated treatment. Indicative from this, too, is that pastoral training itself has provided a framework through which the pastors guide their interaction with people. This also implies that when a patient presents symptoms that may need treatment through psychological assistance, the pastors will, while referring the patient, provide religious treatment for the afflictions. Invariably, this indicates that the pastors may view the client as requiring some form of spiritual treatment for the symptoms presented.

6.1.3 Pastors who are unsure

Participant 4, 7 and 8 had no experience of spirit possession and were unsure in their evaluation and diagnosis of the case study. Participants 4, 7 and 8 were from a German Pentecostal background. However, the uncertainty presented by the participants may be linked to the uncertainty presented by the mental illness in the case-study, which shows symptoms that are similar to a spirit possession. Participant 8 stated: *I could imagine that one could flow into the other. Because there can be similar manifestations. If it is always the symptoms which ultimately give information about where the problem comes from, that is also the question.*

Based on the literature review, religious and cultural expression of spirit possession could be discussed here, i.e. that the respective culture in which the church is situated is not to be underestimated (Belz, 2009; Gaw, 1993; Pfeiffer, 1999) and that the culture possibly influences religious practice more than vice-versa. This would also explain why the topic of spirit possession is better known to both of the African interviewees, irrespective of their denomination (whether charismatic or Baptist), and is more likely to be diagnosed, as the results in the table presented.

6.2 Theme 2: If it is a mental illness, how do they proceed?

Participants 1, 2, 3, 5 and 9, who assumed mental illness, basically stated similar steps as to how they would proceed, i.e. how they would help the person seeking advice. All were German pastors. While participant 1 would ask for more information in order to find out whether possibly occult practices in the past could be behind the voices, participants 2, 3 and 9 view going to a psychologist as more important. According to their own opinion they are not trained to deal with mental disorders.[59] Participant 1 stated: *I'd first of all probably try to listen and find out if he often heard these voices and try and find out if there were situations in his life where he'd been preoccupied with evil spirits or occult practices; so to listen and find out if he might know where it comes from, or if he is having treatment for mental problems, so to see if there is a background to it.*

Participant 9 stated: "*Here I would try and find a possibility for therapy straight away, someone the person could trust and who I knew had professional training. Spontaneously I would speak of a schizophrenic development here and the man urgently needs help, since this is dangerous. I would really spend time with him, listen to him, take him seriously. Here I would, as a counsellor, reach my limits, even with the training that I have. I think I would understand his abnormal illness and would refer him to an appropriate therapy. It depends a lot on how he interprets the phenomenon himself, if he has integrated it into his faith and thinks that the devil is speaking to him, then I would speak to him as a theologian and say I want to take that seriously and I will pray for you for deliverance, and we don't have to do that ten times, once is enough, otherwise I wouldn't be taking Jesus seriously. Then I would anoint him with oil and then refer him on immediately to someone who could give him therapy.*

6.3 Theme 3: If it is demon possession, how do they proceed?

Three interviewees diagnosed spirit possession, number 6 (German, charismatic), number 10 (African, charismatic) and number 11 (African, Baptist). When the statements of the three participants are compared, it becomes clear that, although they are from different cultures and different free churches (charismatic and Baptist), their procedure based on the same diagnosis is consistent: Prayer. Participant 9 states: *That is why I would always accompany treatment with prayer, but then in a simple way, a prayer is said that concerns the patient and then anointing with oil in order to place the power of Jesus upon that person and that must be enough, and then*

59 Section 6.4 covers in more detail the training of the interviewees in connection with spirit possession and mental illness.

to make accessible all forms of therapeutic help, as long as they are really good, to help this person, that is how I would do it.

Deliverance ministry in the name of Jesus would set the person free from the spirit that is trying to make him commit suicide. Participant 6 from Germany mentions some assumptions for possible reasons as to why the spirit has entered into the person, namely that the person opened himself in the past to an evil spirit, possibly through occult practices. Participant 6 stated that *generally all the work of the devil is built on lies and the Bible says that Jesus Christ has come to set us free, he said that you will receive truth, you shall recognise or comprehend or come to know or experience the truth and the truth shall set you free. So if people believe lies about themselves or about reality, they open themselves up for problems.*

The 'lies' about oneself that participant 6 speaks of, refer to psycho-social experiences that within the discipline of psychology will be met with various conclusions regarding ones well-being dependent upon these experiences. Participant 6 further stated *if you believe you are ugly, that will determine a lot of things, and how you view life. If your parents have always told you that you are evil or that you are incapable of managing life, your self-worth will be damaged. And it is in these damages usually that the influence of evil spirits starts to work on and seek entrance in a human life.* This is important here, because again, the participant alludes to referencing the individual's well-being and mental health from within a religious paradigm. Participant 7 stated that in treating the patient diagnosed with spirit possession he *would like to know when it all started, are there indications of the time when this voice comes. It can also be a purely mental thing, it doesn't have to mean he is demonised. I wouldn't exclude anything. Maybe it is a case of a multiple personality disorder, but it could be that he is demonised; you need more background information, when it began, signs, does anything occur to him. I would call for the elders, if he wanted that, and then we would pray for deliverance.*

6.4 Theme 4: Lack of integrated knowledge regarding mental illness and spirit possession

The analysis of the data from eleven participants provided us with insight that they have had no training whatsoever in this specific area neither against a denominational nor a cultural background. That is, regardless of where the pastor was located geographically or the denomination of the pastor – they had not received the adequate training required to appropriately diagnose and treat the individual who presents him or herself with symptoms that describe mental illness.

One needs to take into account that their theological education dates back to between ten and 30 years ago and only the respective theological training institute is taken into consideration. The table below presents that content analysis of the data.

Own education and knowledge about spirit possession and mental illness:

Pastor	Country	Denomination	Educated in this subject	Enough Education on Spirit Possession and Mental Illness?
1	Germany	Baptist	No	No
2	Germany	Baptist	No	No
3	Germany	Free evangelical	No	No
4	Germany	Pentecostal	No	No
5	Germany	Free evangelical	No	No
6	Germany	Charismatic	No	No
7	Germany	Pentecostal	No	No
8	Germany	Pentecostal	No	No
9	Germany	Baptist	No	No
10	Uganda	Charismatic	No	Yes
11	Tanzania	Baptist	No	Yes

Participant 1 stated that *I think a mental illness and demon possession can appear to be very similar; from the effects and symptoms they can appear very similar. People who hear voices or instructions, or people appear to them or they have contact with people who aren't alive anymore and such things. So they can appear very similar*. This sentiment was carried across the interviews with the 11 participants. Despite the similarity in these symptoms, the participants have not received any psychological training that would allow them the opportunity to effectively diagnose a client whose symptoms may require psychological treatment. Participant 1 informed us further that *I think that is very difficult. I think that in psychology, schizophrenia isn't differentiated from possession, because this isn't found in psychology, because simply God is not in this nor in secular psychotherapy. As Christians, we know that it exists from the reports in the Bible and from reports from people. I think how you proceed is difficult. Prayer is a very important thing for Christians, not that we remove it through prayer, but that we ask God to reveal it clearly through his Spirit, if it could be demon possession.* While participant 6 told us that *a multiple personality disorder can manifest itself as demonisation and vice-versa. Similar to schizophrenia, which has been researched into for a hundred years, but they can't find a result. No one knows the background, many guess that there could possibly be an occult background, too, since it often affects people who have or had an occult background. I experienced that in my work placement, although the doctors would contradict me I am sure.* The awareness that participants had regarding the difference between their diagnosis and the diagnosis of a trained medical professional indicates that pastors themselves may doubt their diagnosis, given the similarity between symptoms. Furthermore, there was an acknowledgment that *we should use the diagnostic criteria of psychology to see what schizophrenia looks like. But all in all it's a very difficult task* (Participant 1).

Based on the responses received from participants, none felt that they had been trained enough with regard to spirit possession and mental illness. This is not surprising since pastoral training does not allow for westernised influences in the manner in which patients are treated.

What is surprising however are the two answers from the African participants (numbers 10 and 11). They stated that they had not benefitted from any training in this respect, however they felt they were sufficiently trained. This was an astonishing finding given that the symptoms of the two experiences are so similar. When questioned further it became clear that both had stated, independently of each other, that the Holy Spirit would instruct them in this respect, i.e. would show them how they could proceed in such cases. This on the other hand is not surprising when the charismatic free churches and their teaching on spirit possession are taken into consideration. Here it is claimed, among other things, that for example by using the gift of discernment of spirits one can recognise whether a person is spirit possessed or not. There are however no statements concerning the recognition of mental illness. Thus it is clear why it is relatively quickly assumed to be a case of possession in these circles. In light of the findings that have been presented, the following model was developed.

Model 1: Integration of theological and psychological knowledge systems

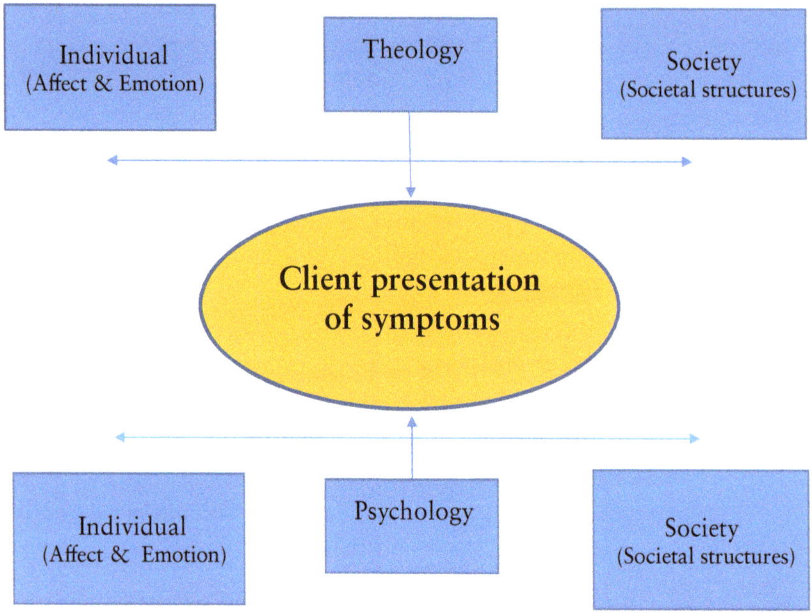

This model essentially represents the interaction between two disciplines, psychology and theology. The need is apparent, given that the treatment of patients who show symptoms of mental illness may not be appropriately diagnosed. Participant 9 stated *when I think of my own course, there was much too little.* Similarly, participant 8 stated *that for quite a few mentally ill people it is attractive to join in with a certain group at least for a certain time, and probably the greater the promises that are made by the church, for example Jesus heals or Jesus makes you healthy, the more such personalities are going to be attracted in the hope that the cure will be found. However, I could imagine that these people wouldn't stay long, if what they are hoping for doesn't happen then they would turn away and continue their search elsewhere.* Participant 7 told us *it would be important for pastors to know where they could get help from. I would find that more valuable than a pastor just having more knowledge about it. The best thing would be to do the same as Jesus: You see the person and heal him holistically.*

It is in line with these understandings that the model was developed. It presents a way of viewing the patient using both the theological and psychological frames of reference. This model allows the pastors to view the patient as being susceptible not only to spiritual ailments, but is subject to psycho-social experiences that could affect mental health. Invariably, the model also postulates that the treatment for a spirit possession may be treated dualistically, using both the expertise and experience of the pastors as well as relying upon psychological knowledge and expertise.

From both a theological and psychological perspective, the individual is seen as having a mutually interactive relationship with society. This in many ways covers the corpus of psychological literature and understanding, which indicate that the person is in harmony with his or her environment. This was indicated to us, for example, by the concept of the "tabula rasa", which clearly was questioned in that as humans we are both influenced by our own genetic make-up as well as environmental influences, while from a theological perspective it is evident and clear that the individual and the society and environment within which he or she resides must exist in harmony. Even though theology is postulated on the premise that society and the individual are dependent upon a higher realm and functioning, that is, the world and the word of God, the individual and the social system must essentially work together to create well-being. In many ways, the individual affect and emotion is influenced by the belief in God. This is stated within the context of this research project, which examines the perceptions of spirit possession and mental illness amongst free church pastors. Therefore, this model excludes any individual who does not locate religion as a core belief.

When a client presents him or herself to a pastor with symptoms that may be diagnosed as being either spirit possession or mental illness, we raise a concern – the issue should not be about the differentiation of the symptoms as being either a mental illness or spirit possession. Rather, the focus should be on a collaborative effort that would allow the patient to receive a holistic treatment plan. This implies enabling the pastors to have adequate information with regards to referrals that they could rely upon. Given that training in mental illness may not be the core focus of pastoral training, this may be a likely solution.

7 Conclusion

This PhD thesis has the title: Free Church Pastors in Germany – Perceptions of Spirit Possession and Mental Illness. It has its origins in intensive personal experiences and research into this topic which ensued from these experiences. There is a great deal of tension between theology and psychology for free church pastors, particularly for pastors in Germany where psychology has effectively overtaken theology. Despite this however, there is a growing need to understand the interaction between psychology and theology especially in light of the experience of spirit possession which brings to call both disciplines.

This topic comprises two disciplines: psychology and theology. The first two chapters were therefore dedicated to both of these areas, namely with regard to how they relate to spirit possession. A first general overview was given here in order to establish the current state of research.

In chapters three and four, the respective psychological and theological theories were outlined. Their particular perspectives clearly show how differently phenomena are treated even when they appear exactly the same at first glance. Explanations and arguments were presented. Based on these results it becomes clear that spirit possession is a complex subject. An initial reason for this is the topic itself, for spirit possession is difficult to grasp and thus difficult to define and according to whether a psychological or theological view is taken, one can arrive at totally different conclusions and strategies (schizophrenia is treated completely differently than if a pastor diagnoses a person as being possessed). This overlap between the areas of psychology and theology presents a major challenge when dealing with the phenomenon of spirit possession. Psychological as well as theological interpretations and explanations of the phenomena are relevant, just as much as the socio-cultural backgrounds and the prevailing belief systems. The methodology was detailed in the fifth chapter and research questions specifically explained in order to answer these in chapter six. As well as showing the current state of research in psychology and theology, the qualitative interviews were evaluated and analysed and a model was developed from the research results. This model points out the complexity of the subject at a glance and one can only guess how difficult it is for free church pastors in Germany to treat spirit possession/ mental illness appropriately and what a challenge they face in this regard.

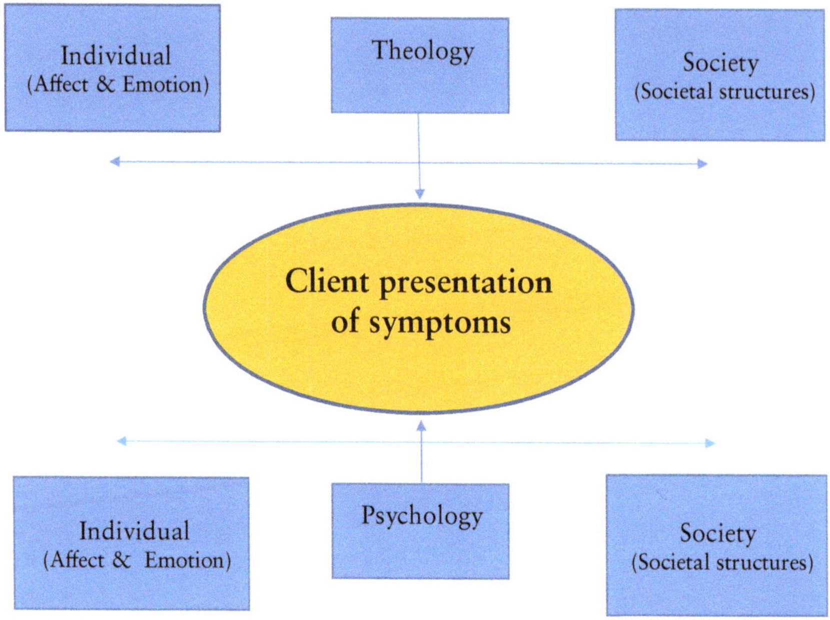

This model shows not only the results of this PhD research project, but also the complexity of the research topic. Whenever people report about their experiences and phenomena, i.e. when they give a subjective description of a phenomenon to someone else, then the latter is presented with a huge challenge, for his own background (affect, emotion, psychology or theology, society) effectively predetermines the counselling method that is to be pursued.

For free church pastors who think and reason spiritually, theologically and biblically, it is not possible to consider something psychologically, therapeutically and scientifically if they are convinced there is no scientific approach to it.

Conversely the same is true for psychologists. These are trained in diagnostics, ICD-10, DSM-5 and so on, know about schizophrenia and personality disorders, but due to these things start out with totally different basic assumptions compared to a pastor (the latter's only resources are his Bible, his experience and the leading of the Holy Spirit).

For this reason, it is not surprising that the results of the interviews turned out as they did. Free church pastors in Germany have little to no specialised knowledge about psychological associations and are thus caught in a dilemma. The question: "Mental illness or spirit possession?" was and is difficult for them to answer. That is why it is necessary in the medium term to introduce this psychological-scientific subject area to theological training institutes. This has been realised in recent years and, as described in Chapter 4, tentatively implemented. This PhD project should help these institutions by making it easier for them to decide to open the door to psychology in their education establishments. Of course not every pastor has to become a psychologist, but merely the information from this research work can provide guidance. Purely theological concepts are insufficient to adequately draw closer to the subject of spirit possession and if people are to be effectively helped, then it appears vital that free church pastors acquire basic knowledge in psychology.

The author of this PhD thesis is already in contact with theological colleges in order to gradually develop appropriate concepts so that future pastors can cope better than their predecessors with the complex topic of spirit possession and mental illness.

Strengths of the study

This study contributed to a growing body of literature by focussing on a very specific group of pastors who work with patients who believe they may be possessed by spirits. In doing so, the study has provided evidence that indicates that more interaction, integration and collaboration between psychology and theology is required. This will provide free church pastors with a deeper understanding of the tension that exists between mental illness and spirit possessions.

In addition, the contribution to the field of psychology is immense. Practitioners need to become more aware of the active role they need to play in providing psycho-education in various contexts and to different professionals.

Limitations of the study

The study is limited in that it focussed primarily on German pastors and their perceptions of spirit possession. Even though two pastors from Africa were included in the sample, the study could have benefitted from more participants.

Secondly, the study could have been enhanced if patients who received treatment from free church pastors were included in the sample. This would have allowed the researcher to comment more on the implication of the treatment patients receive in light of the potential to misdiagnosis.

Recommended Research

The following research is suggested:

1. It would be interesting to investigate this area of tension, in respect of the question of mental illness or spirit possession in other countries with different cultures and religious orientations.
2. Another interesting topic for a research project could be more intensive investigation of pastors in Africa and their experiences of the tension between a diagnosis of mental illness and spirit possession.

Reference List

Al-Issa, I.: The illusion of reality or the reality of illusion. Hallucinations and culture. *British Journal of Psychiatry*, 166, p. 368–373.

Ally, Y.: *Somatic and psychological influence of bewitchment and spirit possession. Exploring differing health beliefs with South African Muslim medical practitioners.*

Ally, Y.; Laher, S. *South African Muslim Faith Healers Perspectives of Mental Illness.* Understanding, Aetiology and Treatment. In: J Relig Health, 47, p. 45–56.

Ally, Y. (2009). *Cultural Perceptions of Psychological Disturbances: The Folklore Beliefs of South African Muslim and Hindu Community Members.* Lambert Academic Publishing: Germany.

Alvarado, C. S. Out-of-Body Experiences. Varieties of anomalous experience: Examining the scientific evidence. In: *American Psychological Association*, p. 183–218.

American Psychiatric Association: *Diagnostic and Statistical Manual of Mental Disorders.* 4th Ed. Washington, DC: APA.

Andrews, L. & Lester, D. Manic depressive tendencies and belief in life after death. *Psychological Reports*, 82, p. 1114.

Arnold, C.E. (1997) *3 crucial questions about spiritual warfare.* Grand Rapids: Baker Books.

Atmanspacher, H., Römer, H., Walach, H. Weak quantum theory: Complementarity and entanglement in physics and beyond. *Foundations of Physics*, 32, p. 379–406.

Baldwin, W. (1991). *Spirit Releasement Therapy: A Technique Manual.* 2nd ed.: The Human Potential Foundation Press.

Banister, P., Burman, E., Parker, I., Taylor, M & Tindall, C. (1994). *Qualitative Methods in Psychology: A Research Guide.* Philadelphia: Open University Press.

Bauer, D.; Lorenz S.; Midelfort E.; Schmidt J.; de Waart H. (2005) *DEMONIC POSSESSION. Interpretations of a Historical-Cultural Phenomenon.* Bielefeld: Verlag für Religionsgeschichte.

Bauer, W. (1971). *Wörterbuch zum Neuen Testament.* 5th ed. Berlin: Walter de Gruyter.

Bauer, E. & Schetsche, M. (2003). *Alltägliche Wunder: Erfahrungen mit dem Übersinnlichen – wissenschaftliche Befunde.* Würzburg: Ergon.

Beck, H. W. (2001). GEIST – WORT – MATERIE. Christus Incarnatus – Herr über die sichtbare und unsichtbare Schöpfung. In: *Hochschulschriftenreihe*, Vol. 9.

Beck, H. W. (1987). *Biblische Universalität und Wissenschaft. Grundriss Interdisziplinärer Theologie.* Neuhausen-Stuttgart: Hänssler-Verlag.

Beck, A. & Miller, J. Erosion of belief and disbelief: Effects of religiosity and negative affect on beliefs in the paranormal and supernatural. *The Journal of Social Psychology*, 14, p. 277–287.

Belz-Merk, M. Counselling and therapy for people who claim exceptional experiences. *Journal of Parapsychology*, 64, p. 238–239.

Belz-Merk, M. & Fach, W. Beratung und Hilfe für Menschen mit außergewöhnlichen Erfahrungen. *Psychotherapie, Psychosomatik, Medizinische Psychologie*, Vol. 55, p. 256–265.

Benassi, V.A., Sweeney, P.D. & Drevno, G.E. Mind over matter: Perceived success at psychokinesis. *Journal of Personality and Social Psychology*, 37, p. 1377–1386.

Bender, H. (Ed.) (1966). *Parapsychologie. Entwicklung, Ergebnisse, Probleme.* Darmstadt: Wissenschaftliche Buchgesellschaft (Vol. 4).

Bender, H. (1973). *Verborgene Wirklichkeit.* 2nd ed. Olten: Walter-Verlag AG.

Berrios, G. Delusions as wrong beliefs. In: *British Journal of Psychiatry*, 159, p. 6–8.

Betty, S. (2007). *Spirit release is a different kind of therapy. Secular healers report promising results.*

Billerbeck S. Strack H. (1928). *Exkurs: Zur altjüdischen Dämonologie.* Kommentar zum NT, Vol. 4. München: Beck'sche Verlagsbuchhandlung.

Blackmore, S. (2007). *Conversations about Consciousness.* Frankfurt am Main: Suhrkamp.

Bose, R. PSYCHIATRY AND THE POPULAR CONCEPTION OF POSSESSION AMONG THE BANGLADESHIS IN LONDON. *International Journal of Social Psychiatry*, 43, p. 1–15.

Bourguignon, E. (1968). *Word distribution and patterns of possession states. Trance and possession states.* Montreal: R.M. Bucke Memorial Society.

Bourguignon, E. (1976). *Possession.* San Francisco: Chandler and Sharp.

Boyatzis, R. E. (1998). *Transforming Qualitative Information.* Sage: Cleveland.

Boyd, A.G. (1997). *God at War: The Bible and spiritual conflict.* Downers Grove: Inter Varsity Press.

Braun, V. and Clarke, V. (2006) Using thematic analysis in psychology. *Qualitative Research in Psychology*, 3 (2), p. 77–101. ISSN 1478–0887.

Brennan, J. F. (1998). *History and systems of psychology.* London: Prentice-Hall International.

Brock, A. C. (2006). *Internationalizing the history of Psychology.* New York: University Press.

Broderick, D. (2007). *Outside the Gates of Science.* New York: Thunder's Mouth Press.

Brysbaert, M., & Rastle, K. (2009). *Historical and conceptual issues in psychology.* Harlow: Pearson.

Bultmann, R. (1948). *Kerygma und Mythos.* Hamburg: Evangelischer Verlag.

Coenen, L. (1993). *Theologisches Begriffslexikon zum Neuen Testament.* 1. Sonderausgabe. Wuppertal: Brockhaus.

Coffey, A. & Atkinson, P. (1996). *Making Sense of Qualitative Data: Complementary Research Strategies.* London: Sage.

Cohen, E. (2008). *What is Spirit Possession? Defining, Comparing and Explaining – Two Possession Forms.* In ETHNOS 73, p. 1–25.

Cuneo, M. (2001). *American Exorcism.* New York: Doubleday.

Dawson, A. (2011). *Summoning the spirits. Possession and Invocation in Contemporary.* New York: Taurus & Co.

Daxelmüller, C. *Besessenheit.* In: Handwörterbuch zur historischen und vergleichenden Erzählforschung, p. 195–206.

de Waart H. (2005). *Dämonische Besessenheit. Zur Interpretation eines kulturhistorischen Phänomens.* Bielefeld.

Demling, J. H.; Thierauf, P. *Zur ärztlichen Einschätzung von „dämonischer Besessenheit". Ein nicht nur historischer Abriss.* In: Wege zum Menschen, Vol. 62, p. 332–349.

Denzin & Lincoln. (2003). *Handbook of qualitative research* (pp. 105–117). London: Sage.

Denzin & Lincoln. (2003). *Collecting and Interpreting Qualitative Material.* London: Sage Publications.

Dickason, C. F. (1992). *Demon Possession & the Christian. A new perspective.* 5th ed. Illionois: Good News Publishers.

Dieterich, M. (2009). *Wie Menschen sich ändern – und was wir dazu beitragen können.* Witten: SCM R. Brockhaus.

Dieterich, M. (2012). *Handbuch Psychologie & Seelsorge.* 7th ed. Witten: SCM R. Brockhaus.

Dieterich, M. & Scheffbuch R., Tlach W., Veeser W. (1986). *Biblische Grenzfragen im Bereich der neueren Spiritualität.* Neuhausen: Hänssler-Verlag.

Dörner, D.; Selg, H. (1985). *Psychologie. Eine Einführung in ihre Grundlagen und Anwendungsfelder.* Stuttgart.

Dudley, R. & Whisnand, E. Paranormal belief and attributional style. *Psychological Reports*, 86, p. 863–864.

Dwyer, G. (2003). *The divine and the demonic: Supernatural affliction and its treatment in North India.* London: Routledge Curzon.

Ellenberger, H. F. (1970). *The Discovery of the Unconscious: The History and Evolution of Dynamic Psychiatry.* London: Fontana Press.

Fiedler, P. (2002). *Dissoziative Störungen.* Göttingen: Hogrefe (Fortschritte der Psychotherpie).

Foerster, W. (1971). *daimon, daimonion, daimonizomai.* Theologisches Wörterbuch zum Neuen Testament. Vol. 2.

Fossey E, Harvey CA, McDermott F, Davidson L. (2002). *Understanding and evaluating qualitative research.* Australian and New Zealand Journal of Psychiatry, 36, p. 717–732.

Freud, S. (1940). *Eine Teufelsneurose im siebzehnten Jahrhundert.* Gesammelte Werke, Bd. 13, p. 317–353.

Freud, S. (1940). *Gesammelte Werke.* 18 Bände. London: Imago Publishing Co. (Vol. 13).

Fugmann, H.; Lamprecht, H. *Besessenheit und Exorzismus aus evangelischer Sicht.* Beiträge zur Erforschung religiöser und geistiger Strömungen, Vol. 10.

Gaw, C. A. (1993). *Culture, Ethnicity and Mental Illness.* Washington, DC: American Psychiatric Press.

Gehrts, H. (1966). *Das Mädchen von Orlach*. Stuttgart: Ernst Klett Verlag.

Geldbach E., Burkhardt H., Heimbucher K. (Hg.) (1986). *Evangelisches Gemeindelexikon*. Wuppertal: Brockhaus.

Grawe, K. (1994). *Psychotherapie im Wandel. Von der Konfession zur Profession*. Göttingen: Hogrefe.

Grawe, K. (2006). Neuropsychotherapy: *How the Neurosciences inform effective Psychotherapy*. Zürich: Lawrence Erlbaum Associates.

Grof, Stanislav (1988). *THE ADVENTURE OF SELF-DISCOVERY. DIMENSIONS OF CONSCIOUSNESS AND NEW PERSPECTIVES IN PSYCHOTHERAPY AND INNER EXPLORATION*. Albany: New York Press.

Grof, Stanislav (2013). *Das Abenteuer der Selbstentdeckung. Heilung durch veränderte Bewusstseinszustände – Ein Leitfaden*. 8th ed. München: Kösel-Verlag.

Grossklaus, M. (2009). Holistic Counselling in Cases of Paranormal Phenomena. Masterthesis.

Guba, E. G., & Lincoln, Y. S. (1994). Competing paradigms in qualitative research. In N. K.

Guiley, R. (1991). Harper's Encyclopedia of Mystical & Paranormal Experience. New York: Harper Collins.

Haraldsson, E. & Houtkooper, J.M. Traditional Christian beliefs, spiritualism, and the paranormal: An Icelandic-American comparison. *International Journal for the Psychology of Religion*, 6, p. 51–64.

Häselbarth, C. (1999). *Befreiung*. Solingen: Gottfried Bernard Verlag.

Häselbarth, C. (1999). *Zur Freiheit berufen*. Solingen: Gottfried Bernard Verlag.

Hergenhahn, B. R. (2005). *An Introduction to the History of Psychology*. Sixth Edition. Wadsworth: Cengage Learning.

Horhershall, D. (1995). *History of psychology*. 3rd edition. USA: McGraw-Hill.

Irwin, H. J. Belief in the Paranormal and a Sense of Control over Life. *European Journal of Parapsychology*, 15, p. 68–78.

Irwin, H. J. Belief in the paranormal: A review of the empirical literature. *Journal of the American Society for Psychological Research*, 87, p. 1–39.

Ivey, G. (1997). *The psychology of satanic cult possession.* Unpublished PhD dissertation. University of Natal.

Jackson, M. Benign *Schizotyp? The case of spiritual experience.* Implications for Illness and Health, p. 227–250.

James, W. (1961). *The Varieties of Religious Experience.* New York: Macmillan Publishing Co.

Jehl, R. (2005). *Melancholie und Besessenheit im gelehrten Diskurs des Mittelalters.* Dämonische Besessenheit, p. 63–71.

Jung, C. G. (1960). *The Structure and Dynamics of the Psyche. The Psychological Foundations of Beliefs in Spirits.* New York: Bollingen Series XX.

Jung, C. G. (1971). *Gesammelte Werke.* Olten: Walter (8).

Kelly, V. A. (1999). *The Curriculum: Theory and Practice.* London: Sage Publications.

Kennedy, E. & Kanthamani, H. (1989). An exploratory study of the effects of paranormal and spiritual experiences on people's lives and well-being. *Journal of the American Society for Psychical Research*, p. 249–264.

Kick, H. A.; Engelhardt, D. von; Gerigk, H.-J.; Schmitt, W. *Besessenheit, Trance, Exorzismus. Affekte und Emotionen als Grundlagen ethischer Wertebildung und Gefährdung in Wissenschaften und Künsten.* Affekt – Emotion – Ethik, Vol. 2, p. 1–217.

Klaas, M. (2003). *Mind Over Mind: The anthropology and psychology of spirit possession.* Lanham: Rowman & Littlefield Publishers.

Koch, K. (1981). *Besessenheit und Exorzismus.* Basel: Brunnen.

Koch, K. (1982). *Seelsorge und Okkultismus.* Basel: Brunnen.

Koenig, H. G.: *Religion, spirituality and psychotic disorders.* Rev. Psiq. Clin., Vol. 34, p. 40–48.

Kraft, H.C. (1992). *Deep Wounds, Deep Healing.* Michigan: Servant Publications.

Kraft, H.C. (2000). *Frei von dunklen Schatten – Grundlage für den Befreiungsdienst in der Seelsorge.* Erzhausen: Projektion J.

Kraft, H.C. (2000). *Ich gebe euch Vollmacht – unsere Autorität im Namen Jesu.* Lüdenscheid: Asaph.

Kramer, W.; Bauer, E. (2012). *Perspectives of Clinical Parapsychology.* Bunnik: Stichging Het Johann Borgman Fonds.

Kramer, W.; Bauer, E.; Hövelmann G. (2012). *Perspecitves of Clinical Parapsychology. An Introductory Reader.* Bunnik: Stichting Het Johan Borgman Fonds.

Krech, D., Crutchfield R.S.; Livson N. (1958). *Elements of Psychology.* Second Edition. Berkeley.

Krippendorff, K. (1980). *Content Analysis: An Introduction to Its Methodology*. Beverly Hills: Sage Publications.

Kvalem S. & Brinkmann, S. (2009). *InterViews: Learning the Craft of Qualitative Interviewing*. London: Sage Publications.

Laborde-Nottale, E. (1995). *Das Zweite Gesicht.* Stuttgart: Klett-Cotta.

Leahey, T. H. (2000). *A history of psychology: Main currents in psychological thought.* New Jersey: Prentice-Hall.

Lechler, A. (1978). *Krankheit oder Dämonie?* 2nd ed. Stuttgart: Goldene Worte.

Lerrick, W. (2001). *Unsere Vollmacht in Christus.* Oberweningen: Koinonia.

Lhermitte, J. (1953). *Echte und falsche Mystiker.* Luzern: Räber & Cie.

Lieblich, A., Tuval-Mashiach, R., Zilber, T (1998). *Narrative research: Reading, analysis, and interpretation.* London: Sage Publication.

Lütz, M. (2011). *IRRE – Wir behandeln die Falschen. Unser Problem sind die Normalen.* München: Goldmann-Verlag.

Maccoby, E. E. & Maccoby N. *Das Interview: Ein Werkzeug der Sozialforschung.* Praktische Sozialforschung, p. 37–85.

Malone, J. C. (2009). *Psychology: Pythagoras to present.* London: MIT Press.

Mallone, G. (1992). *Ziehet an die Waffenrüstung Gottes.* Wiesbaden: Projektion J.

Mario R. & Boeker W. Delusions of witchcraft. A cross-cultural study. *British Journal of Psychiatry*, 114, p. 963–972.

McLeod, J. (2004). *Counselling.* Tübingen: dgvt-Verlag.

MacNutt, F. (1995). *Deliverance from evil spirits.* Grand Rapids: MI: Chosen Books.

Mertens, D. M. (2007). Transformative Paradigm: Mixed Methods and Social Justice. *Journal of Mixed Methods Research,* 1 (212).

Mesulam, M. M. *Dissociative states with abnormal temporal lobe EEG. Multiple personality and the illusion of possession.* Archives of Neurology, 38, p. 176–181.

Midgley, J. (2004). *Social Policy for Development. London*: Sage.

Miller, J. *Textbook of Transpersonal Psychiatry and Psychology*. Psychiatric Services, 49, p. 541–542.

Montgomery, J. W. (1976). *Demon Possession. A Medical, Historical, Anthropological and Theological Symposium*. Minneapolis: Bethany Fellowship.

Moreira-Almeida, A. (2007). *Spirituality and health: past and future of a controversial and challenging relationship*. Archives of Clinical Psychiatry. Sao Paolo: Rev. psiquiatr. clín., vol. 34.

Moreira-Almeida, A.; Lotufe-Neto, F. (2005). *Spiritists views of mental disorders in Brazil*. Transcultural Psychiatry, 42, p. 570–595.

Moreira-Almeida, A.; Lotufe-Neto, F.; Koenig, H. G. (2006). *Religiousness and mental health: a review*. Rev Bras Psiquiatr, 28, p. 242–250.

Moreira-Almeida, A.; Lotufe-Neto, F. & Greyson, B. (2007). *Dissociative and psychotic experiences in Brazilian spiritists mediums. Psychotherapy and Psychosomatics*, 76, p. 57–185.

Moser, F. (1950). *SPUK*. Baden: Gyr-Verlag.

Munger, M. P. (2003). *The history of psychology: Fundamental questions*. New York: Oxford University Press.

Naegeli-Osjord, H. (2007). *Besessenheit und Exorzismus*. 2nd ed. St. Goar: Reichl Verlag.

Naumann, E. *Exorcism Through the Ages*. Philosophical Library.

Newport, F. & Strausberg, M. *Americans' belief in psychic and paranormal phenomena is up over last decade*. Gallup Poll News Service.

Niemann, U. *Das Böse und die Psychiatrie – zur Diskussion über Besessenheit und Exorzismus*. Blickpunkt. Herder Korrespondenz, Vol. 60.

Niemann, U. (2005). *Exorzismus oder Therapie? Ansätze zur Befreiung vom Bösen*. Regensburg: Friedrich Pustet.

Niemann, U. (2005). *Verrückt oder besessen? Menschliche, seelsorgerliche und therapeutische Möglichkeiten im Umgang mit „Besessenen"*. Regensburg: Friedrich Pustet.

Nugent, C. *Masks of Satan – The demonic in history*. Psychological Medicine, 17, p. 21–29.

O'Boyle, Goodenow C. (2006). *History of psychology. A Cultural Perspective*. New York: L. Erlbaum Associates.

Oesterreich, T. J. (1930). *Possession, Demonical and Other*. London: Kegan Paul.

Oesterreich, T.K. (1921). *Die Besessenheit*. Langensalza: Wendt & Kauwell.

Page, S. The role of exorcism in clinical practice and pastoral care. *Journal of Psychology & Christianity*, 17, p. 121–131.

Palmer, T. J. (2011). *A REVISED EPISTEMOLOGY FOR AN UNDERSTANDING OF SPIRIT RELEASE THERAPY DEVELOPED IN ACCORDANCE WITH THE CONCEPTUAL FRAMEWORK OF F.W.H. MYERS*. University of Wales, Bangor.

Pfeifer, S. Belief in demons and exorcism in psychiatric patients in Switzerland. *British Journal of Medical Psychology*, 67, p. 247–258.

Pfeifer, S. *Demonic Attributions in Nondelusional Disorders*. Psychopathology, 32, p. 252–259.

Pfeiffer, T.; Mack, J.E. & et al. (2007). *Mind Before Matter*. Ropely: O Books.

Prince, D. (1996*). Biblische Grundlagen für den Befreiungsdienst sowie Anleitung zum Befreiungsdienst an Kindern und Jugendlichen*. Solingen: Gottfried Bernard.

Prince, D. (2004). *The End of Life's Journey: Sharing Christ's Victory Over Death.Charlotte: Derek Prince Ministries.*

Prince, D. (1998). *They shall expel demons*. Charlotte: Derek Prince Ministries.

Reiband, N. (2010). *Klient, Therapeut und das unbekannte Dritte. Placeboeffekte in der Psychotherapie und was wirklich wirkt*. Heidelberg: Carl-Auer-Verlag.

Richards, G. (2002). *Putting psychology in its place: A critical historical overview*. London: Routledge.

Rome, H. P. *Reflections on the concept of multiple personality*. Psychiatric Annals, 14, p. 15ff.

Samuels, A.; Shorter B.; Plaut F. (1986). *A Critical Dictionary of Jungian Analysis*. London: Routledge & Kegan Paul Limited.

Scala, M. (2012). *Der Exorzismus in der katholischen Kirche. Ein liturgisches Ritual zwischen Film, Mythos und Realität. Regensburg*: Friedrich Pustet.

Schmaus, M. (1941). *Katholische Dogmatik*. München: Hüber Verlag.

Schnell, R., Hill, P.B., Esser, E. (2008). *Methoden der empirischen Sozialforschung*. 8th ed. München: Wissenschaftsverlag.

Shiraev, E. (2011). *A history of psychology. A global perspective.* Thousand Oaks: SAGE.

Simon, L. (1996). *William James Remembered.* University of Nebraska Press: Lincoln and London.

Sims, A. Demonic influence and mental disorders. *Journal of Psychology & Christianity*, 8, p. 35–48.

Sims, A. (1986). *Demon possession: Medical perspectives in a western culture.* Exeter: Paternoster Press.

Somaundaram, D.; Thivakaran, T.; Bhugra D. *Possession States in Northern Sri Lanka.* Psychopathology, 41, p. 245–253.

Stafford, B. (2005). The growing evidence for "demonic possessions": what should psychiatrist's response be? *Journal of religion and health,* 44, p. 13–30.

Stevens, M.J., & Wedding, D. (2004). *Handbook of international psychology.* New York: Routledge.

Teuffenbach, A. von (2007). *DER EXORZISMUS. Befreiung vom Bösen.* Augsburg: Sankt Ulrich.

Unisa, department of psychology (2009). *A guide to masters and doctoral studies in psychology*, Pretoria. Unisa.

Unterste H. (1977). *Theologische Aspekte der Tiefenpsychologie von C.G. Jung.* 1st ed. Düsseldorf: Patmos Verlag.

Vaitl, D. (2012). *Veränderte Bewusstseinszustände.* Stuttgart: Schattauer.

VandenBos, G. R. APA Dictionary of psychology, p. 747–753.

Veeser, W. (2013). *Mit psychisch kranken Menschen in Beziehung sein. Hinweise für Angehörige und Gemeinden.* Holzgerlingen: SCM Hänssler.

Von Lucadou, W. (1997). *Geister sind auch nur Menschen – Was steckt hinter okkulten Erlebnissen?* Freiburg: Herder.

Von Lucadou, W. (1997). *PSI-Phänomene. Neue Ergebnisse der Psychokineseforschung.* Frankfurt am Main: Insel Verlag.

Von Lucadou, W. (2012). *Die Geister, die mich riefen.* Köln: Bastei Lübbe.

Vufford, R. K. Demonic influence and mental disorders. *Journal of Psychology & Christianity*, 8, p. 35–38.

Wagner, C.P. (1993). *Wrestling with Dark Angels*. Solingen: Gottfried Bernard.

Walach, H. *Generalisierte Quantentheorie (Weak Quantum Theory). Eine theoretische Basis zum Verständnis transpersonaler Phänomene*. Freiburg.

Warner, T.M. (1991). *Spiritual Warfare*. Wheaton: Crossway Books.

Weyel, B.; Gräb, W. (2006). *Religion in der modernen Lebenswelt. Erscheinungsformen und Reflexionsperspektiven. Religion und Psychologie*. Göttingen: Vandenhoeck & Ruprecht.

Wilkinson, T.(2007). *The Vatican's Exorcists. Driving Out the Devil in the 21st Century*. New York: Hachette Book Group.

Word Health Organization (1992). *International Classification of Diseases*. ICD-10. 10th Ed. Geneva.

Wright, J.S. (1974). *Der Christ und das Okkulte*. Erzhausen: Schönbach.

Zellinger, A. (1978). *Das Rätsel des Bösen*. Stuttgart: Goldene Worte.

Zutt, J. (1972). *Emotion and Possession*. Bern: A.-Francke-Verlag.

Appendix

I Questions guideline for the interviews
II Case Study[60]

Appendix I

Questions guideline for the interview

Can you tell me about yourself?

What are the types of experiences that you face in your ministry?

Tell me about spirit possession (what is it? How does it happen? Who are the most vulnerable and why? What are the symptoms? What causes a spirit possession?).

What is your understanding of a mental illness? (what is a mental illness, how does it "look", how does it affect the person, how many people have you seen with a mental illness? What causes a mental illness?).

I let the pastor read a <u>case study</u> (man with inner voices which speak two times a week saying "jump from a quarry")...

What do you think about it, what is the problem, what would you do...?

Are there any similarities between a spirit possession and mental illness?

What are these? How do you distinguish between the two?

What is schizophrenia?

If the symptoms of the two experiences are similar, it must be a challenge to identify which client has been possessed and which client requires mental treatment, how do you differentiate?

60 Personal Communication, 05/06/2010.

Appendix II

Case Study

A middle-aged man speaks with the pastor after the church service. He tells him that he has been hearing a voice inside him for several months. It speaks to him normally about twice a week and commands him to drive to the quarry near the village where he lives and plunge down into it.

www.ingramcontent.com/pod-product-compliance
Ingram Content Group UK Ltd.
Pitfield, Milton Keynes, MK11 3LW, UK
UKHW061932100926
8556IPUK00007B/877

9 783631 698518